equALLY

equALLY

Stories by *FRIENDS* of the Queer World

Editors

Srini Ramaswamy
and
Ramkrishna Sinha

First published by
Rupa Publications India Pvt. Ltd 2021
7/16, Ansari Road, Daryaganj
New Delhi 110002

Sales Centres:
Allahabad Bengaluru Chennai
Hyderabad Jaipur Kathmandu
Kolkata Mumbai

Copyright © Pride Circle 2021
The copyright of the individual pieces vests with the respective author.

The views and opinions expressed in this book are the authors' own and the facts are as reported by him/her which have been verified to the extent possible, and the publishers are not in any way liable for the same. Names of some people have been changed to protect their privacy.

All rights reserved.

No part of this publication may be reproduced, transmitted, or stored in a retrieval system, in any form or by any means, electronic, mechanical, photocopying, recording or otherwise, without the prior permission of the publisher.

ISBN: 978-93-90547-76-0

Second impression 2021

10 9 8 7 6 5 4 3 2

The moral right of the authors have been asserted.

Printed at Saurabh Printers Pvt. Ltd, Noida

This book is sold subject to the condition that it shall not, by way of trade or otherwise, be lent, resold, hired out, or otherwise circulated, without the publisher's prior consent, in any form of binding or cover other than that in which it is published.

Contents

Introduction	*vii*
Anjali Gopalan	1
Argho Sen	4
Aruna Desai	7
Ashish Kumar Jha	11
Dilip Chenoy	14
Ernesto Noronha	18
Gunveen Ahuja	21
Harish Narayanan	26
Hemal Shah	28
Ishita Katyal	33
Dr Jyotsna Suri	36
Kanak Sahoo	38
Karan Virwani	41
Kevin G. Kochar	44
Koushumi Chakraborti	48
Madhavi Dahanukar	51
Meetul Patel	55
Mishkkaa Verma	62
Mohit Malhotra	64

Mohit Shukla	66
Nandita Das	69
Dr Nilakshi Roy	73
Nitya Bhalla	76
Nivruti Rai	79
Pankajam Sridevi	82
Pavan Vaish	85
Payal Pasha	88
Ramkumar Narayanan	91
Sanjay Murdeshwar	95
Saptorsi Hore	98
Shaina Shingari	102
Simar Singh	105
Sindhu Gangadharan	110
Sreekanth Arimanithaya	114
Sudhir Shenoy	117
Sudish Panicker	122
Dr Sukanyya Misra	125
Suneeta Rao	129
Surekha Shenoy	132
Tanisha Vinod	136
Tanvi Choksi	139
Taru Dahiya	143
Tina Muthanna	146
Trinetri Arora	148
Vedica Saxena	150
Acknowledgements	155

Introduction

We have often been asked what it takes to be part of the LGBT+ movement and why allies matter to the LGBT+ community. The fact is, neither of us—Ram and I—is an activist, working tirelessly on the ground across our large nation. Nor are we lawyers who know how to address the law in courts, arguing for LGBT+ rights.

In effect, we have been beneficiaries of the work put in by activists, scholars and lawyers that saw the reading down of Section 377 and verdicts, such as the NALSA judgement of 2004, in favour of trans rights.

Our education at best, prepared us for the corporate world—a space that we have grown very familiar with while working our way up, Ram as a techie and I, as a human resource professional. We saw talent come and go. We saw freedom at the workplace for some, as well as the stifling of identities particularly of those who belonged to the LGBT+ community.

As Ram and I grew in our careers, our paths crossed time and again at conferences where diversity and inclusion (D&I) was in focus. Ram identified himself as gay and had grown to openly carry his sexual identity with him. Being a heterosexual man, I did not need to speak about my sexuality, after all, I belonged to a majority that had rarely paused to think of how the 'normative' had impacted the lives of sexual minorities.

Every time I met Ram and several others from the queer world and listened to their journey; what they sought; how they felt left out, unsafe and stifled, I realized my advantages and why there was a lot to be done in an area I was familiar with—the workplace.

These many interactions led Ram and I to set up Pride Circle with the initial purpose of bringing social change starting from the workplace. Ram represented the lived experience of a gay man and I emerged as an ally. An ally, I learnt, can help reduce a tiny bit of the emotional and mental baggage that the LGBT+ people are compelled to carry, by being a voice, a support, a lending hand, standing up when it matters, and pushing the system into a direction of inclusivity through policy and culture.

As Ram once told me, the heterosexual world takes so much for granted, not realizing how the unsaid and unstated safety was always theirs and not for the LGBT+ people. "You wouldn't know what it means to be embraced for who you are when you are different, when 'fitting in' becomes a primary task for so many, living in denial of who they are for days, months and years," Ram said.

In other words, if an ally wishes to carry the responsibility of being an ally, they have to emotionally embrace the LGBT+ community. This means making an LGBT+ person feel 'equally' safe, where the ally 'fits in' to the world of LGBT+, literally removing the distinctions of 'us' and 'them', becoming part of each other's lives.

Like anyone else, LGBT+ people exist as children, part of families, students, executives in a company and so on, emphasizing the need for allies and a support system across the spaces they 'live' in. In a way, the requirement is a circle of pride, covering the many touchpoints that life is lived in.

Introduction

When we set out to put this book together, we realized there were so many allies out there, in all of the above-mentioned 'spaces' of life. What was missing, was a reference point, a piece of literature to record such stories and history, a collection that could reassure the world that there is still some good happening, even if it is not reported in the media. We believe that this anthology—as is the case with stories—can influence mindsets, give hope and even motivate some to make a choice of being an ally by putting humanity first, and living together as this book says—Equally.

Srini Ramaswamy,
Co-founder, Pride Circle

Anjali Gopalan
Human Rights and Animal Rights Activist,
Founder, Naz Foundation

My journey with the LGBT+ community started 25 years ago, when I set up the Naz Foundation in Delhi. The purpose behind the foundation was to curb the spread of HIV, make people—largely men having sex with men (MSM)—aware of safe sex, sexually transmitted diseases (STDs) and infections. This meant that I was bound to interact with a very vulnerable population of gay men.

These interactions were not limited to sexual health only. Almost every conversation dealt with stability of the mind, safety at home and in society, the search for love and acceptance and all the fears harboured by these men. I was both a listener and a counsellor to them, someone whose home could be their safe space for the few hours they spent with me, or as part of the group meetings organised by my NGO on the first floor of my home office.

The more I got to know them, the more friendships I cultivated within the Pride rainbow. This allowed me the good fortune of having an extended family. And this was probably why I found it difficult to accept the discrimination that the LGBT+ community faced at the hands of society and Section 377. From my fieldwork and research, it was evident that this section of the IPC was used as a tool for harassment. Policemen would corner volunteers leading safe-sex programmes and accuse them of criminal acts even when all they did was distribute condoms to encourage safe sex. Mind you, such programmes were part of a larger initiative of the government—National AIDS Control Organisation (NACO) in particular.

During my work, I came across many gay men who were being forced into heterosexual marriages. Even when the parents knew their son was gay, they insisted that he should get married to a woman, and use his spare time to meet other men. While that itself was absurd and oppressive, no one thought about the plight of the woman stuck in such a marriage.

However, what shook me the most was an incident sometime in the year 2001. One day a boy walked into our office. I remember him saying: "I don't know what to do. I am being given shock treatment." His parents had reached out to doctors to 'convert' him to heterosexuality. Such treatment was legitimised not at some obscure clinic, but at a major hospital in South Delhi.

That is when we approached the National Human Rights Commission (NHRC) to bring it to their notice. But they said that men having sex with men was a criminal activity, so the only way out, of course, was the reading down of Section 377. This is what led to our petition being filed in the Delhi High Court in the same year.

While the journey of that legal battle is well documented—with a victory, finally, in September 2018—it was one that constantly reminded me of the prejudices that are deeply ingrained in our society. The case showed us how the innocence of love and care is stolen from our childhood with the imposition of fixed definitions of being a boy or a girl, of love and hate, normal and abnormal, acceptance and rejection, and every binary that distances us from each other.

Anjali Gopalan

Over the years, the last two decades in particular, I doubt there has been a Christmas, a New Year's party or any special festivity at home that has not had its bit of 'queerness' (a word that I got familiar with, only in the past five years). I find it hard to think of the sexual minorities within my extended family of friends as 'them' or the 'other'. I find it difficult to think of them beyond their loving ways, flaws, quirkiness and pain.

This is why I find the word 'ally' to be extremely new and strange. All I have been is a friend to people from the LGBT+ community and they have been nothing more than loving friends to me.

Argho Sen
Head Commercial Products,
Service and Operations, India
Natwest Group

Two years ago, I joined the LGBT+ workstream as the Rainbow Network sponsor.*
This was after India's Business leadership team decided that each of the company's diversity initiatives should have a senior sponsor. I have always been a liberal and supportive in my efforts towards inclusion of the LGBT+ community.

Now, working with a team of young, enthusiastic volunteers who share the same mindset and values, has further expanded my awareness about the LGBT+ community. I am thoroughly enjoying my additional role as senior sponsor of the Rainbow Network.

My approach towards this new role was from an organisational perspective. I wanted the Rainbow Network team to adopt fresh goals which would amplify the overall impact of its work through its various advocacy and outreach activities. So, we zeroed in on two goals: To create a safe and inclusive working environment for LGBT+ colleagues and to become an employer of choice for the LGBT+ community.

---

[1] Rainbow Network is the Pride ERG (Employee Resource Group) at NatWest India.

To achieve our first goal, we developed a 'Myth Buster' pack for our colleagues in India.

Personally, this was quite a learning curve. I used the pack to run myth busting sessions for senior leaders in India, which had a positive impact. These helped us debunk the myths and stereotypes associated with the LGBT+ community. We even amended our existing policies and made them LGBT+ friendly. This, in turn, made our workplace even more inclusive. The modified policies now include benefits like same-sex partner medical aids, all gender and orientation inclusive Prevention of Sexual Harassment (POSH), inclusive parental leave policies for adoption and surrogacy, all access to restrooms for transgender colleagues and more.

For me, the biggest learning in this journey has been to gain an understanding of the challenges faced by the transgender community in India. Most of them either drop out of school or run away from home, which leaves them with limited options to build a better future for themselves. We are proud of the support we offer to this community. For our second goal, that is, to become an employer of choice for the LGBT+ community, we designed an exclusive Transcend Internship Programme in 2019 which has received a positive response. Under this programme, we offer a three-month on-the-job training experience. The programme has also helped us to reassess our hiring practices to make them more inclusive.

However, there were some challenges to this approach. For many in the community, corporate internship was the first experience of its kind. Moreover, there were confidence and communication issues which were later improved with professional and personal development programmes. This was a minor hiccup. All said and done, we now have our first intern who has joined NatWest Group India as a permanent member!

Our aim is to encourage a diverse and inclusive work culture, and to make the LGBT+ community more visible within the organisation. There is much to do here and we will continue to improve this further.

I firmly believe we are on the right path to champion the potential of the LGBT+ community. After all, this is how we aim to live by our purpose where all employees experience a sense of belonging at the workplace.

Aruna Desai
Co-founder,
Sweekar–The Rainbow Parents

I remember the time when my son came out to me as gay. I was familiar with the term 'gay', but I did not understand it completely. I poured out whatever I had in my mind in response to his coming out to me. I then went on to ask him whether this was something permanent. I wanted to know if there was absolutely no possibility of him being with a girl. However, while I had these questions, I was certain that I still loved my son just as much as before. His coming out did not change anything for me in that sense. I pondered over it for a while and concluded—if he had told me about him being gay, something that is not accepted as normal in society, it meant that he trusted me and was confident that I would understand him. I could not break his trust. This prompted me to ask him more questions to grasp what he felt and what it meant to be gay. My son was patient with me during this phase and also shared books and articles on the topic of homosexuality. I even researched over the internet about the same.

Now when I look back, I realize the one thing that I did right was to accept my son and not slip into denial that a lot of other parents do.

A common question that a lot of parents ask their children when they come out—what if you are not able to find a life partner?

In my case, when my son came out to me, he already had a partner. So, the issue of not being taken care of in my old age did not bother me. But when he had his first break up, all those fears came rushing back to my heart. It took me some time but I was able to convince myself that I should trust him and have faith that he can take care of himself. I had to accept that he can be happy and single at the same time, and that I should be happy for him as well, regardless of whether he had a partner or not. I completely acknowledge that as parents we have hopes and dreams for our children, and that is totally understandable. But at the same time, it is critical to remember that our children are their own person. We cannot put the burden of our expectations on them. They have their own hopes, dreams and desires. We must stand by to support them in achieving these.

Children from the LGBT+ community often have a hard time accepting themselves. So as parents, we should not make them feel worse in any way. We need to understand their internal struggle when they feel no one is on their side. We need to focus on being non-judgmental, rather than accusatory. I am not saying that this is an easy or a natural thing to do. But this is something we need to work towards—no matter how uncomfortable it makes us feel, or how difficult it looks. We never left a stone unturned while nurturing our children despite all challenges and obstructions. So, why give up now?

Based on my own experience of being a parent to a gay son, I have created a list of Dos and Don'ts for individuals who might be starting their own journey as parents of LGBT+ children.

I would recommend:

1. Observe to what your child's life is like, and what kind of experiences they have had in the world.

2. Take the time to seek information about the lives of LGBT+ people from parents of LGBT+ individuals and friends of your child. Please read up on the subject. Talk to your child.
3. Respect your child's right to engage in loving relationships.
4. Try to develop trust and openness by allowing your child to be who they want to be without any pressure.
5. Defend them against discrimination.
6. Support your child's individual goals, even though they may differ drastically from your own.
7. Say "I love you" very often.

Some things that I would advise against are:

1. Holding your child responsible or blaming your child for your own feelings.
2. Rushing the process of trying to understand your child's sexual orientation or gender identity.
3. Assuming that your child should see a professional counsellor or encourage them to participate in 'reparative therapy'.
4. Criticizing your child for being different.
5. Trying to break up loving relationships.
6. Trying to force your child to conform to your ideas of proper sexual behaviour.
7. Blaming yourself because your child is gay, lesbian, bisexual or transgender.
8. Demanding that your child should live up to your idea of what a man or woman should be.
9. Forcing your own life goals on your child.

Most of all, I believe that the most reassuring thing you can say is, "I love you, and I am proud of you for trusting me and opening up to me." Become an advocate for family and friends.

equALLY

Reiterate your care and love. Ask what you can do to provide support. It is a difficult journey, but it is worth it.

Ashish Kumar Jha
Director-Automation Solutions,
Invesco

Somewhere in 2015, I remember I was out for drinks with a close friend to watch the India versus Bangladesh cricket match at a trendy sports bar in the city. India had won and our spirits were high. Soon, the channel changed to the news where the animated anchor spoke about politics and more on what was happening in the country. Shortly, the topic shifted towards the LGBT+ community. I was watching and listening carefully when my friend interjected, "This is all fashion. They wear these masks and appear to be cool. This is just a facade. It isn't real!"

His remarks made me furious and I dived in to share my two cents on the subject. This resulted in a heated debate over the LGBT+ issues in the country and the existence of the community. I told my friend to refrain from passing such remarks when he did not know anything about it at all. This incident also brought back memories of an old school friend. I faintly remember that was in 2001, when we were in class 10th. He was a close friend of mine, very shy. He was not participative in all the boyish rants and games. Still, he was part of our cricket team. On one fateful day, when we were out to play a zonal match at KV Salt Lake, he came out to me. I, of course, did not know much about it, and I don't think I gave him the support he needed.

The row at the sports bar and the remorse of not having done justice to my friend propelled me to do something about it. "Better late than never," I thought. I started reading about the topic. I even called up a professor of mine to get the right resources and educate myself about the LGBT+ community. With over a decade of global exposure on account of work, networking and leisurely travel, I knew about the community, but I was certain that my superficial knowledge and understanding will not suffice anymore. So I wanted to dive deeper.

Fortunately, I found access to a lot of literature including the National Legal Services Authority (NALSA) judgment on the inclusion of the transgender community, and the high court and Supreme Court judgments, apart from the literature from various UN agencies. I also stumbled upon an employee resource group (ERG) which focused on diversity and inclusion (D&I) initiatives. I invested enough time on it and, by 2016, I could see the beginning of my journey towards becoming an ally.

At my workplace, I announced myself as an open ally. I opened my door to anyone and everyone who wanted to talk about the LGBT+ community and discuss their thoughts on the same. Soon, I attended Pride walks, round tables and any other related event that I could participate in. I raised questions about the D&I initiatives restricting themselves to gender and not addressing the entire spectrum of sexuality. Before long, we were conducting LGBT+ awareness sessions at our company. Teams representing Invesco were there at NASSCOM D&I Council, Pride Circle events and eventually hiring folks from RISE (Reimagining Inclusion for Social Equity) Job Fair. Our workplace gradually became more inclusive and welcoming, from gender neutral washrooms to gender neutral policies. We had it all in place.

I think it was the little extras that went a long way in helping us build trust. Every Friday, I wore a T-shirt to work that said 'Pride without Prejudice'. I even had a placard in my office that said 'Love is Love'. I firmly believe that these small things helped me win the confidence of my colleagues and encouraged them to confide in me. Gradually, they knew they could come to me and share their stories with me. I was proud to be able to earn their trust. Soon, I was receiving requests from people outside the company seeking my help in understanding what it takes to come out at the workplace. They wanted to know the pros and cons of coming out, whether it hampers growth at work and so on. And I must say, I have been really lucky to mentor and guide a few bright young individuals who have shown some spark.

From my experience, I can conclude that engagement with the community starts with empathy and it needs to go beyond policy or organisational boundaries. As an ally, it is not one's job to be a therapist or counsellor. It is one's job to listen to the LGBT+ people in their life and at the workplace, ask them how they have been doing and be aware of what they may have gone through (and/or might still be going through). It is not so much about understanding everything that a member of the community goes through, but about extending support in every way possible. The most important thing is to keep our minds and hearts open beyond events and round tables.

Dilip Chenoy
Secretary General,
The Federation of Indian Chambers
of Commerce & Industry (FICCI)

Economies across the globe are moving towards inclusion. Truly inclusive economic development can be realised when all sections of society are able to participate in the overall growth trajectory. In the case of the LGBT+ community, society and the corporate sector are required to facilitate the community's integration in economic development so that its members can live with a sense of freedom and security. A focussed approach towards the community's inclusion will also empower them both economically and socially.

Many members of this community are forced to hide their true selves fearing repression or discrimination. As members of a global community, we must make efforts to secure protection, rights and respect for the LGBT+ community.

I strongly feel that if we care about making society and our own workplace truly inclusive, we can bring real change—as an ally. FICCI is openly allying with the cause of LGBT+ inclusion at workplace and encouraging corporate India to become more diverse, inclusive and better for all—including the LGBT+ community in India. At the workplace, an LGBT+ person's merit should weigh more than their sexual identity. Organisations should foster an inclusive environment where each employee feels respected, valued and involved, irrespective of their caste, gender or religion.

I feel honoured to say that with representations from leading corporate firms of India, FICCI is the first apex industry association in the country to set up a dedicated Task Force on Diversity and Inclusion (D&I). This task force has a focussed subgroup on LGBT+ which has been organising awareness sessions, thematic webinars and consultations with the government, multilateral agencies, corporates, NGOs and other stakeholders to bring the voice of the LGBT+ community to the table.

Several studies have proven that inclusion has economic benefits too. FICCI was associated with the launch of Open for Business and Boston Consulting Group's report titled 'New Global Champions: Why the fastest growing companies from emerging markets are embracing LGBT+ inclusion'. The revenue growth, earnings before interest and taxes, and international revenue of 96 high-potential emerging-market companies were analysed in the report. The survey findings show that a growing number of companies are focussed on LGBT+ inclusion and that these companies can more effectively globalise.

By including members of the LGBT+ community in society and giving them respect, we can enhance productivity, reduce mental health issues and witness a higher contribution to the country's GDP. (Increased individual productivity leads to collective growth of the country's productivity and hence higher contribution to GDP.)

More and more corporates in the country have now started taking initiatives to become more diverse and inclusive. There is also a special focus on enhancing livelihood opportunities for transgender people through corporate social responsibility engagements. Through the D&I task force, FICCI wants to champion a no-fear work culture where everybody can feel included.

Here are a few suggestions which could be instrumental in instilling hopes and pacifying apprehensions of the LGBT+ community and advancing their participation in the mainstream:

- To address the issues related to homophobia at work and fuel right opportunities for the LGBT+ people, organisations must encourage empathetic communication at all levels to raise awareness about LGBT+ rights. This will ensure a non-discriminatory approach towards accepting the LGBT+ people as their true selves.
- It is also advisable to create network support mechanisms such as employee resource groups within organisations to enable LGBT+ people to reach out to a friend/mentor. This will give them an opportunity to connect deeply with each member and share their issues and vulnerability.
- Even experience sharing sessions coupled with community inspiration stories can play a great role in building effective allies and creating safe workspaces.
- Corporates must also come forward to showcase their growth story as an LGBT+ ally to inspire others and seed catalysts of positivity.

Being the voice of the Indian Industry, FICCI has been instrumental in bringing about many policy changes through several active sectoral committees and stands committed towards building an inclusive nation by stimulating a robust D&I agenda across India Inc.

I would like to conclude with a quote by Harvey Bernard Milk, the first openly gay elected official in the history of

California, US: "It takes no compromise to give people their rights. It takes no money to respect the individual. It takes no political deal to give people freedom. It takes no survey to remove repression." This quote continues to be relevant in today's world.

Ernesto Noronha
Professor,
IIM Ahmedabad

WAKING UP TO THE WORLD OF LGBT+ PEOPLE

My encounter with the LGBT+ community dates back to my early childhood when I saw friends in my locality teasing 'hijras' who came to attend or participate in auspicious ceremonies. Their existence was also used by parents and elders to discipline children like me. I was warned: "Go to sleep or else the 'hijra' will come and take you away." On other occasions, I realised that effeminate men were labelled 'hijra' as they did not fit the masculine gender expectation and were ridiculed for their effeminate demeanour. I realised that being a male meant being macho and strong. Any deviation from these norms invited similar marginalisation or ridicule. For instance, whenever I cried as a child, I was immediately called a 'sissy' or a 'girl'.

However, other people enacting gender roles which were not in sync with the social gender expectations did not bother me. So, I grew up without a clear understanding about the hijra community, and I accepted them as being part of the social system without judging their behaviour or sexuality.

My first close interaction with a gay person took place in college where gay people were often joked about. However, I did not bother to dig deep into the issue. Other encounters occurred when I travelled to the US and met gay partners of relatives at family gatherings. I woke up to the issues concerning the gay community much later. This was when a gay colleague of mine was outed by another heterosexual colleague in one of my previous workplaces. I was shocked and flummoxed to know that there was a buzz about somebody's sexuality at the workplace.

It so happened that my gay colleague decided to come out by posting a blog about his sexuality. Until then, none of us knew about his sexuality since the general stereotypes associated with gay men did not apply to him. He was well respected for his capabilities. Nonetheless, once he was out, another heterosexual colleague took it upon himself to inform others about this colleague's sexuality. To convince others about what he had unearthed, the person would open our colleague's blog in which he came out as gay in front of other colleagues.

I felt awkward when confronted by this gossip. It did not matter to me if my colleague was gay, but I was concerned about him being outed by another colleague. My gay colleague could have emailed the website link to all of us if he wanted us to know about his sexuality. Even though I was unhappy about what was happening, I was not sure about how to intervene. Meanwhile, the gossip monger began to portray his homophobia and conveyed that he wanted me to avoid our gay colleague. He would say, "Don't sit near him, you will get AIDS!" I ignored him and showed my irritation at times with this uncalled-for advice. My wife Premilla D'Cruz's research with people living with HIV/AIDS patients helped me understand all about the transmission of AIDS better.

Since 2015, I have been teaching a course on diversity which tackles discrimination against the community. As part of the course, the first talk on LGBT+ issues at IIM-A was open to the entire institute.

Subsequently, IIM Ally, an LGBT+ resource group at IIM-A, was formed, which was officially recognised on campus in 2017. It has been hosting talks and generating awareness in IIM-A. I have just completed a research project that shows how the LGBT+ community overcomes fear in the workplace.

Gunveen Ahuja
Head of Contact Center, Bangalore,
Pride India Lead, HSBC

I was born in a small town in Punjab, the land of five rivers, the food basin of the country.

Chandigarh is right in the middle of three states, geographically as a well as culturally. It is a small town with a very high per capita income. Hence, it has a history of being rich but has people with a constrained mindset.

My upbringing was happy but conservative. Thanks to my education, I had the opportunity to broaden my horizons and look beyond my immediate surroundings and beliefs.

In my late 20s, I moved to Mumbai, a melting pot of cultures and diversity, which was completely different from my hometown. I started working as a communications and culture trainer for Hero Mindmine Ltd. The sheer number and diversity of people I met and worked with grew exponentially, bringing about a drastic, and much needed change in my mindset.

A few years later, I took up my first corporate role in a customer experience centre, where I built my early years of learning as a Training and Transactional Quality (T&TQ) expert, and then later in another organisation as a People Leader.

In 2008, I joined IBM as a customer experience leader, where I led a large and diverse team to success. I was with the company for three years and managed some great outcomes and mentored some great talent. I got mentored in people leadership skills under some very good leaders.

This was followed by a strong leadership stint at American Express and a short one at Flipkart e-commerce. I am now a senior leader with HSBC, handling a 1000-member contact centre (which happens to be one of their largest contact centres in the world), managing three markets and multiple products. My large and diverse team that I swear by is the reason for my success as a leader.

I have always been very sensitive and empathetic towards people whom I saw being discriminated against. My earliest memories of discrimination were the ones that were faced by the 'hijra' community. They survived by singing and dancing on auspicious occasions in Indian households. I had limited understanding of their sexuality and used to wonder about their complicated appearance and their source of livelihood. I could never understand the ridicule that they faced at the hands of our society, when what was most needed was compassion and inclusivity. Yet, in complete contrast, they were and still are deemed to be lucky and their blessings are sought by all. The irony!

Later in life, I came to know about alternate sexuality. I was curious about such people but never found them to be any different from myself, and was disgusted with how society treated them as if they were abnormal. People discriminated against them blatantly, in families, workplaces, educational institutions and even in the fine arts.

This has forced members of the community to hide so much. When I made friends who belonged to the community, the feeling of partnership and camaraderie grew even stronger.

While it took India 71 years after independence to repeal

Section 377 of the Indian Penal Code which prohibited consensual sex between members of the same sex, it is taking a bit longer to remove historical cobwebs. This movement of acceptance of the LGBT+ community is gaining ground and inclusivity is becoming the new norm among leading organisations and multinational companies. However, a lot more remains to be done to change people's mindsets and their preconceived notions.

As the world opens up, so should our minds and hearts. Every day, newer categories are discovered and added to the LGBT+ family. We need to embrace every view, every person and protect everyone from social oppression as well as other forms of attack.

I see myself as a strong and lifelong 'Ally' in this effort. I have always been sensitive and supportive, but now I believe my commitment to this cause has grown beyond just being that. I cannot recall any specific incident, that made me who I am today. Thanks to my exposure to global teams and people, I have been exposed to the possibility of a much more open world than the one we live in today. My friendships and acquaintances go beyond just sexual identity now and make me a powerful ally.

Today, I lead the Pride initiative for HSBC India and have spearheaded various initiatives like Amplifying Pride (formal launch of India Pride ERG), Pride March for HSBC employees, participation in #RoadtoRISE (twice) – a comprehensive job fair exclusively for the LGBT+ community, #21DaysAllyChallenge secured the 5th position (where 158 organisations had participated).

I have won numerous leadership awards and have recently been instrumental in enabling HSBC India win the coveted IWEI (India Workplace Equality Index) recognition and

Spotlight Award, internal HSBC UK award for nurturing a diversity and inclusion (D&I) mindset at site level and creating an environment of inclusivity.

Through my personal life and career, my learnings and beliefs have been carved into the following core values:

- Do not judge people. Trust them by default and then let the relationship evolve.
- People, by default, want to help others. Bring that out in them to drive great customer and employee experiences.
- Values always take precedence over competence. Always. Intent can be magical.
- There is no skill that cannot be learnt. That is why they call it a skill. Talent is a different story.
- Discrimination over identity, race, religion, sexual orientation, gender identity, physical ability or any other classification has no place in civil society, or organisations, or this world.
- Customer is the number one priority. They pay—we stay.
- In God I believe, and my teams, I trust. For everything else, there is data.

Due to my diverse background (conservative upbringing versus liberal education), some people from my past find it tough to have a similar mindset and thus react with caution. However, through constant education, awareness, normalisation and conversation, it is getting better for people to understand this community. The fundamental belief that "Competence, intent and ability, and attitude is all that matters", is gaining ground.

The best part is that, the current and future generations are much more aware of, accepting and normal about diversity as compared to us and our elders. In that sense, they are teaching us so much about it! Any phobic or offensive behaviour is met with so much disdain that one has to be careful always. That is the power of the youth. I firmly believe we are on the road to success, and I am definitely a part of the winning team!

The LGBT+ movement is not a just a movement for equality or rights. It is a metaphor for freedom. Freedom to choose, freedom to live, freedom to love. Also, to be open to newer sections joining the movement every day as curiosity piques and information increases.

And to be in it for life—all the way. And wear it on your sleeve, with PRIDE.

I will repeat one of my values here:

"Discrimination over identity, race, religion, sexual orientation, gender identity, physical ability or any other classification has no place in civil society, or organisations, or this world."

Harish Narayanan
Head of Marketing,
Myntra

From the beginning of my professional journey, I have been extremely fortunate to be part of extraordinary companies which had a deliberate and deep focus on diversity, inclusion and acceptance. During my stint in Singapore and then later in India, I experienced first-hand what it meant to actually implement the principles of acceptance and that has remained ingrained in my approach towards diversity and inclusion.

I am a very inquisitive person by nature. Whenever I meet someone new, I am excited and curious because it is a chance for me to step into a completely fresh perspective and look at humanity through a new lens. Hence, empathy towards everyone—irrespective of who they are or where they come from—has always been natural to me.

But, while I never held negative views about the LGBT+ community, I was not an advocate either. My journey towards becoming an ally and eventually an advocate happened over years, bit by bit—there is not one particular incident that I would call transformative. It started with some interactions I had with a few friends, who shared their stories with me. Listening to their stories was an eye-opening experience. They spoke about their everyday struggle for acceptance and love; their dreams of getting married to someone they love and having children, things that a 'normal' person like me takes for granted. As my exposure increased, I understood more. I also learnt to modulate my vocabulary. I asked a transgender friend about their preferred pronoun, and I now ask about a colleague's 'partner' instead of assuming 'wife' or 'husband'.

I have come to realise that if my voice can help even one person feel at ease with who they are—at my workplace or outside—then I will ensure I voice it.

In my interactions with people from the LGBT+ community, I always tell them to share their stories boldly and invite others to step into their world. They should know they can find strength in the community. My advice to them is, "Know you are not alone, speak up and be heard, look out for the helpers."

And to the rest of you, who are not part of the community but want to help, become an ally. Gender identity and sexuality may be complex topics, but love and empathy are very simple. Start by doing what I did initially; listen patiently, put yourself in their shoes, maybe even shed a tear or two in the shared pain. And then, let them know you are there for them, amplify their voice when you can and speak up when you see discrimination or oppression. We Indians are champions at "unity in diversity" having been taught, "All Indians are my brothers and sisters". We never bat an eyelid when we befriend people who look different, speak a different language, eat different food or worship different Gods. Then why should this be any different?

Hemal Shah
Asia Pacific CIO, and SVP of Data, Dell Digital

One of my fundamental beliefs is that we always make progress as a team. Though an introvert at heart, I am very passionate about people. I believe in pushing myself and I like people who go the extra mile to make a difference.

During my time in the US, I had heard about the LGBT+ community but did not personally know anyone from the community. Back then, I saw how tough it was for people from the community to be accepted as their authentic selves. Knowing that a lot of people felt the need to hide an intrinsic part of themselves from society gave me cause for concern. This is when I felt things needed to change. I would not want to be a part of any organisation or community where people are not accepted for who they truly are as individuals.

Years later, I had another 'aha!' moment that gave me an opportunity to make a meaningful impact towards this cause. My true involvement started when Erik Day Senior Vice President and General Manager, Small Business and Pride ERG Global Executive Chair at Dell Technologies), reached out to me to discuss the wonderful work being done by the Global Pride Employee Resource Group (ERG) at Dell Technologies. He asked me if I would be willing to sponsor the India Pride ERG.

That night, while sitting at the dining table with my family and discussing this, my children educated me all about the LGBT+ community. They felt it was such an awesome opportunity, "Dad, you must do this!" They even suggested that I speak to some of their friends to understand it better. I was surprised to see how much more open-minded the younger generation is. To me, that was a huge inspiration and that was the moment I said to myself, "Okay, now I'm absolutely doing it!" Such reinforcement from your children really helps. This was my tipping point. It is one thing to accept change, but it is a whole different experience and responsibility to lead from the front and drive the change.

Having understood how important it is to be an ally (and how much my children valued me doing it), I was more than happy to take up the responsibility. This opportunity has made me a lot more aware about the community and I am a strong believer that everyone should become an ally.

At Dell Technologies, we strive to create a work environment where differences are valued and everyone has an opportunity to succeed. Our 'Progress Made Real' Social Impact vision for 2030, includes a focus on cultivating inclusion and creating an environment where everyone feels they can be their true, authentic selves.

It is my belief that nurturing an inclusive culture which is representative of our diverse, global customers could help create positive change outside the workplace as well. It is by understanding, valuing and embracing the diversity of our team members that we can understand our customers better. Furthermore, it also helps to spark innovation through a more diverse range of ideas and experiences, empower our team members and ultimately gain competitive advantage.

equALLY

Studies have shown that team members perform better and produce better results when they are able to bring their real selves to work. It is simple—when people are authentically being themselves, they are much happier and more productive. In this way, we are more likely to attract and retain top talent.

I am proud to be the executive sponsor of the Pride ERG in India along with P. Krishnakumar. We launched the official charter of the Pride ERG in 2017. It was a huge success for Dell India to invite and encourage all team members and leaders to join the network, and collectively work towards supporting our LGBT+ team members and community. Our APJ (Asia Pacific Japan) Pride sponsor at the time, David Webster, participated in commemorating the launch of our India chapter along with 500+ team members.

As one among 13 ERGs and with over 400 ERG chapters around the world, Pride ERG India has come a long way in these last two years. With the Pride ERG, we have supported policy change and delivered medical benefits for same-sex partners. We secured benefits for transgender team members across the APJ region and worked to make our offices and facilities inclusive with gender-neutral washrooms across all sites of Dell India. We are also focussing on advancing awareness with our Pride Ally certification initiative, and growing our Ally numbers.

Dell's presence at both the Pride Summit and Zinnov D&I Confluence in 2019, showcased our thought leadership in establishing LGBT+ inclusion in the corporate workforce. Dell has also co-sponsored a research publication on 'LGBT+ Workplace Inclusion in India' by Community Business. Additionally, Dell represented Pride India in the 'Out & Equal 2019 Conference'. To celebrate Pride Month in 2020, we joined Pride Circle for the #21daysAllyChallenge virtual campaign which focused on building a community of passionate LGBT+ Allies.

Our efforts for FY21 involve plans to further enhance our benefits, build strong allies within the company and increase community engagement activities on a continual basis to have a positive impact on our team members and the community. While we are very proud of the work we have done in driving progress across our communities, we recognise that more work is needed, and we will continue working on our commitment, leading by example.

Becoming an ally also helped a lot on the personal front. I have been able to engage in meaningful dialogue about the community, with many people belonging to different age groups. I am glad to be able to share my experiences with them. The ability to make even a small difference in some people's lives, not just the children but their parents too, through my individual efforts gives me immense satisfaction.

Being an ally, it opened up my scope for improving the hiring process and making it more inclusive. I am more comfortable now to educate people about biases and pre-conceived notions, both at the workplace and outside it.

We all look different, think differently, talk in different languages and are incredibly diverse in so many ways. Life is all about knowing how to accept and respect each other for our similarities and differences alike. I love the determined attitude of the people who are part of the community, "Hey look! This is what it is". They keep fighting barriers. That is the right attitude and there is nothing wrong about it.

The true test of diversity and inclusion is when we no longer need to talk about it as an initiative but accept it to be the norm. Every step towards equality took the enlightenment of a few individuals, and the transformation of a few generations

equALLY

before we emerged as a more inclusive and progressive society. I am committed to continuing their work and making change happen—are you?

Ishita Katyal
Author and Public Speaker

I am 15 years old. For close to five years now, I have been working very passionately to inspire the youth around me. I want to create a positive impact and spread awareness about how everybody is unique. I have always believed that it is very important for my generation to understand that we need to create opportunities for ourselves and others around us and start working on what we love to do from an early age.

I strongly believe that age is just a number and no matter how old you are, you can always create a wave of change. For me, it is always the little things in life that matter the most and I think we should strive to make the best out of the limited resources we have at hand.

I became a deep-rooted ally roughly two years ago, when I made an effort to educate myself about the LGBT+ community. I remember that from Grade 5 onwards in school, some of my friends would be teased just because someone was not behaving in the conventionally masculine/feminine manner. It had become so common to hear words like, "Oh, you're acting so gay!" or "Oh! You're acting like a lesbian" around me. As a child, I did not really understand what these terms meant, or what the LGBT+ community stood for, so and I asked my parents what it meant. When they explained it to me, I did not really have a problem with it. In fact, my close circle of friends and

I actually found the concept to be very beautiful. So we were shocked when we realised there are so many people who were not accepting of the LGBT+ community, and that pushed me to become an ally. I did a lot of research and read up on coming out stories, gender identities, usage of pronouns and more. I felt that while there will always be people who will oppose the community, if I could spread some positivity at my level that would be great. It made me happy that I could use my voice to stand up for others and be there for them.

I mean, everyone has their likings and preferences, so why do some people have to be so judgemental about the LGBT+ community, which has different sexual orientations when it comes to romantic relationships? The saying, "Love is love" is so apt. Who you love, is up to you as an individual and no one should make that decision for you.

As humans we all have pre-conceived notions that we have grown up with because of societal conditioning. But we need to learn how to be accepting. The kindest and the smallest contribution that one can make is to just listen (with an open heart!). It is really that simple—just be there for someone, hear them out and try to understand what they are feeling. Empathise with them as we are all unique and we all deserve the same opportunities, no matter who we identify as.

After being a visible and vocal ally, a few friends of mine who were closeted came out to me and expressed what they were feeling and that gave me such happiness. To know that they trusted me with such a significant detail of their life and knew that I would understand them and not disclose their identity brought me such a sense of self-love too. It is like contributing to someone's life in the smallest way.

I also realised that most of the negative reactions I received

Ishita Katyal

when I spoke up for the community were due to misinformation or unawareness. And once I was able to explain to these people exactly what the LGBT+ community stood for and the struggles they faced, most of them wanted to learn more and be allies themselves.

From my experience, I can vouch that the voices and thoughts of the LGBT+ community are purely filled with positivity and I don't think there's any negative side to spreading love for a cause that's just for the larger welfare of everyone in this world. Ultimately, it is just about spreading awareness and correcting the misinformed. I mean what can be bad about helping people to be more accepting? And breaking the barriers of gender and societal stereotypes?

For the allies that are just starting out, commend yourself that you have made an effort to become informed. Take a stand for any act that you feel is not right. Put your voice out there and educate yourself more and more about the LGBT+ community.

If my generation were to join hands and unite it is only going to be a great future ahead.

Dr Jyotsna Suri
Chairperson and Managing Director,
The Lalit Suri Hospitality Group

My journey as an LGBT+ ally is deeply personal. Fifteen years ago, my son Keshav came out to me. I took close to twenty-four hours to absorb the revelation and, thereafter, accepted Keshav for who he is.

When the Hon'ble Supreme Court read down Section 377 of the Indian Penal Code, the landscape for the LGBT+ community changed for the better. The onus is now on the people of India to change their mindset. They need to break the stereotypical image of the community that they have in their minds, accept them socially and mainstream them—professionally and economically.

While legal protections are important, much more is needed for the LGBT+ community members to live with dignity and without discrimination. This is particularly important for young people who experience estrangement from their family and friends, making them most vulnerable. Their harassment at school often leads to them dropping out of school and with mental health issues. The community also suffers from socio-economic inequalities due to discrimination at the workplace. Legislative failure to protect the LGBT+ community denies them their basic fundamental right for a better and safe environment.

Dr Jyotsna Suri

The Keshav Suri Foundation was launched in 2018 with the motto to embrace, empower and mainstream the LGBT+ community. The foundation is affiliated with the 'It Gets Better India' programme and provides an online forum to the community members so that their voices can be heard. As a mother, I am really proud of Keshav for making it better for himself and endeavouring to make it better for others as well. It is because of him that I have learned about and understood the extremely marginalised LGBT+ community.

The Lalit Suri Hospitality Group has established itself as one of the most inclusive and safe spaces in the country, providing a conducive working environment for all individuals. The group has undertaken numerous steps to educate and sensitise its teams about the LGBT+ community. It has also forged a partnership with Federation of Indian Chambers of Commerce & Industry (FICCI) to create a platform to table and discuss the challenges faced by the community.

Being an ally for the community means recognition, respect and equality for its members.

I urge you all to accept, empower and mainstream the LGBT+ community.

Be an ally!

Kanak Sahoo
Parent and Homemaker

The impact of a child coming out can be far more intense on mothers than anything else. Our society has always considered mothers to be the moral guide for their children. Mothers also tend to take the blame for anything that happens in their child's life. And that is why such revelations can really push any mother deep into the abyss. For me, it was absolutely shocking because I had no prior knowledge or awareness about the LGBT+ community. I had never even thought about what it meant to be gay. I remember I had cried for almost a month when my child came out to me. It was a difficult and lonely journey since I could not cry in front of my child. I never wanted him to feel guilty for making me cry.

All the while, I kept worrying about society, friends, family and my son, Anwesh's own future. I was constantly stressed about it. However, when I started reading about the subject, it started getting slightly easier. I began to understand him. Anwesh also helped me in this by making me aware of the various issues and the psychological aspects of it. I always knew that he is my child and no one can understand him better than me, his mother. It just took some effort and direction to embark on that journey.

In retrospect, I still feel sad that he was all alone in his journey of self-acceptance. Though I am proud he did it and became the fabulous person that he is, the fact that he could not find courage to come out to me sooner still hurts. I wish I was there for him and could support him more.

I completely agree that for parents, it is not an easy process. They need time to comprehend and respond. Most of the parents have never heard of these terms and have never imagined anything else outside of what societal constructs have offered them. They will need time to understand. However, I feel it is important for parents to be supportive when their child comes out to them, even if they do not understand it completely at the moment.

Take your time, but till then, never neglect your child. Be there for them. Never make your child feel they are not normal. Society can be very different for them, to an extent cruel too. You are their strongest ally. They can face the questions and deal with them gracefully only if you accept your child unconditionally. This is important for their happiness. They will be more confident, more open and would do well in all spheres of life. Respect your child. Never abandon them.

For me, nothing has changed after my son came out to me. Yes, the journey has been long and arduous but I love him and he loves me too. He is my child. I am his mother. That is it. If he is happy, I am happy. That should be the only thing that matters—his happiness. I never judge him and I have been very lucky with regard to my family and friends too. They all have been very supportive. No one has ever taunted me or passed a negative remark. Luckily, his friends in his engineering college also encouraged him to talk and be open about it. My daughter is also very supportive and I am proud of the way she took a stand for her brother by refusing to get married in a certain family that had no acceptance for my son.

There have been instances when people have commented

about my son being gay (not normal, different). I have often wondered about this and I sincerely want the term LGBT+ to demolish. Why do we need a separate label? Why can we not address them as we address everyone else? Labelling them makes things worse. It constantly makes them aware that they are secluded and not included.

Respect and treat them as humans. God has created them and He cannot be wrong. Who has given us the right to put them in isolated groups? Who are we to judge them and to categorise them as right and wrong? If you look into mythology or even ancient history, you will understand that gay people have always existed. They are not a new species. It is us who have forgotten them.

I strongly believe that gender studies should be a part of the school syllabus. Every child should know and study about it. This should really be the 'new normal'. No judgments, no seclusion and no harassment. This is the only way to end the discrimination and make our society a better place.

Karan Virwani
CEO,
WeWork India

WHAT BEING AN ALLY MEANS TO ME

Every time Pride Month ends, we are faced with the question, "Has our commitment to the LGBT+ community changed?" My commitment to the community has not changed—I am an ally, and those words have never been truer than they are today. The year 2020 brought with it enormous change, several setbacks and unprecedented growth. As we adjusted to the new normal, some longed for the certainty of the past, but I saw this as a time for change. In the middle of a global pandemic, we as a society are simultaneously battling a social crisis leading to a restructuring in what it means to be inclusive. The age of discrimination and intolerance is over.

To further understand why being an ally is so important in my own personal journey, one has to account for my professional journey. Before venturing out on my own, I worked with my father at Embassy Group. During this journey, I began to notice that our millennial entrepreneurs lacked nurturing. When I first walked into a WeWork space in New York, I realised the importance of building sound, high quality and large workspaces for corporates and knew it would really connect with Indian millennials who were looking for community, acceptance, collaboration and an outlet for their creativity.

On becoming the CEO of WeWork India three years ago, the inclusivity of the queer community and my mission to be an ally came into stronger focus. The sense of community that is woven so deeply into the fabric of WeWork has no room for discrimination. The energy and vibe one feels by walking into a WeWork building is one of love and acceptance and we wanted to ensure the same sentiment echoed through all our locations. My journey in becoming an ally was inspired by the fact that as a leader and a young CEO, I wanted to ensure that I set an example of acceptance, inclusivity and diversity.

In January 2020, we put our commitment into even stronger practice by extending the company's medical insurance benefits to same-sex domestic partners. This gesture is a testament to WeWork's commitment to acknowledging and celebrating, diversity and inclusion among our more than 350 employees. It was a proud moment for me as CEO, as it established us as the first collaborative workspace provider in the country to offer health insurance covers to partners of all LGBT+ employees. In 2020, to emulate and showcase the vibrant and energetic experience of Pride Month, we launched a microsite that digitally recreates the annual Pride parade, complete with a city street and slogans. Members of our community shared and continue to share messages of love and support which are displayed for everyone to see. This is WeWork's culture put on full display—loving, supportive, open and full of spirit. I hope we as a community continue to break glass ceilings and ignite change.

Professionally, I have been able to work with our teams and the WeWork community to support our LGBT+ colleagues and the society at large, but the journey of becoming a steadfast ally is also a personal one. It started with my own education on the appropriate terminology and the struggles the community faces on a daily basis. I aim to listen more than speak, and when I do speak, it will be to speak out against prejudice. I have pledged to initiate dialogues with friends, members, colleagues and leadership teams to share our learnings and keep the conversation going around the community.

Our country has taken steps towards acceptance with the Supreme Court delivering two historic judgements for the LGBT+ community: the National Legal Services Authority (NALSA)'s judgement of 2014, which recognised the fundamental rights of the transgender community and the abolishment of Section 377 of the Indian Penal Code, which criminalised same-sex acts. There is, however, still work to be done. The most powerful part of taking a stand is that each one of us has the opportunity to be an ally along with being a powerful and driving force in the inclusion of a deeply marginalised community. My initiatives in the workplace are just a stepping stone to a much bigger promise. I urge other leaders, CEOs and business owners to step up and make a change wherever possible. We have been given a platform to influence, encourage and take a stand against discrimination and hatred. We must use it. Progress is more important than perfection. Even a small step in the right direction can light a spark of change.

Going forward, my commitment to being an example of this allyship will go deeper, as there is much more to be done and a lot more change to be seen. I hope you will join me in this endeavour.

Kevin G. Kochar
Managing Director,
Goldman Sachs

In the words of George Bernard Shaw, *"There is eternal war between those who are in the world for what they can get out of it... and those who are in the world to make it a better place for everybody to live in".* My guiding principle in life has been to continually strive for the latter.

My professional journey as a visible advocate of LGBT+ inclusion in Bengaluru started when I signed up as a mentee for the Reverse Mentorship Program at Goldman Sachs, where an out-professional mentors a senior leader by sharing their experience as an LGBT+ professional at the firm. By sharing their personal and professional experiences as a queer individual in India, my mentor played a key role in cementing my personal commitment to make a difference in the organisation.

As a managing director and 25-year member of Goldman Sachs, I have found creative synergies between my personal and professional network to drive progress towards LGBT+ inclusion. I have been involved with the Bengaluru LGBT+ Network as a regional head for a few years now. In this role, I have made it my conscious priority to promote a culture of LGBT+ inclusion in both my business area and the broader firm. In 2018, when the Supreme Court of India read down Section 377, I was elated on many levels, especially since I witnessed the journey of one of the petitioners, who was a former employee and network member. While the change in the legal landscape has empowered LGBT+ individuals in India, they still face a myriad of biases.

Understanding the impact of visible and vocal advocacy, I took it upon myself to become a 'Managing Director Ally' to drive the message of and the agenda on LGBT+ inclusion among senior leadership, and create an increasingly inclusive workplace for our LGBT+ employees. This began with displaying a visible 'Ally' sign and the Pride flag in my office and having an open dialogue on LGBT+ inclusion with senior leadership at the firm. I am proud of the visible culture of inclusion that reverberates in the office.

I am extremely fortunate to be working for a firm that has been a trailblazer for LGBT+ inclusion for more than a decade in India. Goldman Sachs provides a range of inclusive benefits and wellness offerings including gender agnostic sexual harassment policy, gender neutral washrooms on campus, same-sex partner benefits, gender affirmation surgery insurance coverage, resilience offerings and parental leave of 26 weeks irrespective of gender and caregiver status.

I am committed to continuing my efforts towards carving the path of inclusion for LGBT+ professionals at the firm globally. Being part of this journey has helped me become a better leader and further broadened my horizons as an individual. Let me share a few personal highlights:

- Through the firm's 'Community TeamWorks' initiative, we partnered with an external organisation and hosted interviewing skills training workshop for 30 transgender individuals as part of their career upskilling program.
- Alongside other leaders, I have conducted initiatives through the years such as 'Straight Talk', which is a

facilitated dialogue hosted by senior leaders to demystify gender stereotypes and build awareness.
- As part of 'Pride Month' celebrations in November every year in India, we hoist the Pride flag and the Transgender flag in our office campus. It is a pleasure to have other companies and external individuals from the community join us over the years for the flag hoistings ceremonies.
- The Pride Month of 2019 was even more special with the launch of our 'Pronouns Initiative', where employees through various avenues could share their self-identified pronouns. We also hosted a Pride Carnival in collaboration with community partners to raise awareness, and engage colleagues through interactive activities and education.

I believe in the power of the collective conscious, especially with social reform. To drive this agenda forward in India, we sponsored four LGBT+ Inclusion Workshop Series, hosted by NASSCOM, as part of their broader Diversity and Inclusion Summit, across Chennai, Hyderabad, Mumbai and Delhi through 2018–2019. I travelled with my team across these cities to interact with industry leaders and community partners from across the country, which reinforces the importance for everyone to join hands in moving the needle.

In our multicultural society, there are a limited number of role models who have thrived through adversity. So I feel the responsibility to channel my energy and efforts to empower people to have a fair chance to succeed. Allies along with members of the LGBT+ community together in solidarity, can redefine the way the community is perceived and accepted in India.

Kevin G. Kochar

An individual once asked me, "How do you have time to wear multiple hats?" For me it is as simple as, you make time for what you believe is important—and to me, having a safe space to be oneself is paramount. I want to lead by example to create a community of individuals who can challenge the status quo and are not afraid to speak their truth. My advice to fellow allies would be, "Always say something specific, if you see something suspicious".

Koushumi Chakraborti
Senior Lead - Compensation and Benefits, Infosys BPM

I am a mother to an intersex child. I have always embraced the fact that my child would need a lot more support from me, having always reassured them that they will have my complete support and unconditional love forever. Whatever life throws at us, we are a team and will fight it as a team. The only rule in our team is unconditional love and constant unfailing support.

Right from the beginning I was very open about my child being intersex and that irked a lot of people. They said I was interfering with my child's privacy and that I should not announce it publicly. I thought about it very differently though. I always felt that people keep only such information private which they find embarrassing or shameful. I am neither ashamed, nor embarrassed. I am rather proud of my child, and keeping this as a secret from society would only send a wrong message to my child. When anyone asks me if my child is a boy or a girl. I have a standard response—they are intersex. Some understand, while most don't. For me, people's opinions do not matter. My child's well-being and their self-respect does, and I know my priorities.

Moreover, I hope my answer at least makes them aware that intersex children do exist. My child is just as much a part of society as other children. This is why I am vocal about it on all social media platforms. I want people to open their minds to understand what intersex means and to accept them for who they are, without conditions. At the end of the day, if I can help even one parent connect with their intersex child, I would be happy.

I want to tell this to every parent: Whether your children are intersex or not, they are your children. If you would pause for a moment and think about it, being intersex is just one aspect of your child. There are so many other areas of their lives and personalities. They are a whole human being—may be extremely intelligent, great in studies, sports or arts! Your child may be shy and finds it difficult to socialize. Your child maybe confident and spirited. Being intersex does not take any of that away from them or make your child any less of a human being. It is just how they are built anatomically and how they identify themselves from the perspective of 'gender' and whom they are attracted to. Once you have acknowledged this, it will become easier for you to find out more about what your child is thinking, how they are feeling, why they are choosing the identity they identify with and what are the challenges they are facing (physical, psychological and social).

There is really a lot that you can do. Read on the internet, join support groups online or offline. Talk to other parents or other LGBT+ children and/or adults to get a better understanding of how you can help your child. I truly believe that a parent is as old as their child. There is no need to panic or be too hard on yourself as a parent. It is okay to not know everything or anything, immediately. It is important to be open to understanding, learning and un-learning. It is important to listen to our children and not just hear them.

equALLY

Our society, including our immediate close circle of people, does not make it easy for our children or us either. Things can change overnight even with those who may have been their best friends till that moment. There can be taunts and ridiculing in schools or other spaces. Children are vulnerable and ill-equipped to handle all the stress on their own. That is where your role as a parent particularly comes in.

Keep your eyes, ears and heart open to your child's needs. There will be times when your child will express vocally about what they want, but sometimes they may not say anything about what is hurting them. Sometimes, children may not fully understand what they are thinking or feeling as they are learning about their identity one moment at a time. If they know that they have a 'safe person' in you and that their home is a 'safe space', things will slowly begin to fall in place, and life will gradually return to its normal rhythm.

We always evaluate our children on how good they are doing in studies, sports or other areas of life. But let us also evaluate ourselves. We need to ask ourselves the following questions:

Do our children trust us completely?

Do our children know and believe that we are there for them, no matter what?

If the answer is 'yes' for both, trust me, it will be all okay. Just believe in your and your child's goodness. Everything else is manageable.

Madhavi Dahanukar
Country Executive and CEO,
Northern Trust India

MY STORY—A PROUD ALLY TO THE LGBT+ COMMUNITY

It was a cold, winter night in India 20 years ago. We had just finished a quarterly business review with our American client. Sheetal (name changed), who had been hovering outside my office for some time had finally caught my attention. I stepped out and asked him to come inside. He asked if he could close the door as he wanted to speak to me privately.

The next four hours would be the most memorable and defining moments of my life. Sheetal narrated his life story and poured his heart out to me. He wanted my assistance in approving a one-year sabbatical to go to the US for gender affirmation surgery. He needed the organisation to support him with the sabbatical and provide financial assistance. I need to add here that the HR policies did not support sabbaticals at that point in time and insurance/health policies did not cover gender affirmation surgery. However, our organisation was very supportive of the request and Sheetal got most of what he asked for.

A few months prior to Sheetal's return, we created a small support group to sensitise the broader teams at the office on what to expect after Sheetal returned. Two years later, Sheetal was back at work. This Sheetal was different from the Sheetal we knew before she left for the US, in more ways than her gender. She was more cheerful, more fun, and in her own words, "Finally able to be myself".

I have a lot to thank Sheetal for. She touched a chord in my heart. When I look back and think of how my support for the LGBT+ community came to be, I always go back to that cold, winter night! That conversation, and the resultant reflection, helped me build a new perspective—one of empathy, appreciation of diversity without bias and judgement, and to celebrate the world for all its different elements, as that is what makes it so beautiful.

A lot has been said about diversity, equity and inclusion (DEI) in the workplace and, in the past few years, there has been demonstrable evidence of the financial benefits for organisations that are more diverse, equitable and inclusive compared to those that are not big on DEI. The business case for both gender and ethnic diversity is robust and applies globally, across countries. However, the LGBT+ community has not had the same level of focus. It is estimated that 8-10% of the global population identifies as LGBT+; if that is how our societies are made up, shouldn't that be how our workplaces are made up as well?

As we look to rebuild our organisational cultures amid the current crisis caused by the COVID-19 pandemic, we have a unique opportunity to reaffirm our commitment towards the DEI agenda, especially keeping the LGBT+ community in mind.

It is our responsibility to make our organisations look like the world we experience outside our workplaces. If our products and services are consumed by people from all walks of life, we must ensure they are designed by a diverse set of people who bring a broad range of perspectives for consideration. Diversity drives greater innovation and that is a proven fact.

Some thoughts for consideration:

- Redefine gender diversity—Why do we restrict our definition of gender diversity to only women? Can we broad base the conversations around gender to include people from the LGBT+ community whose gender identities are non-binary in the larger spirit of embracing the diversity spectrum and being truly inclusive? There is no denying that progress has been slow with respect to bringing women into the workforce and most firms focussed on the DEI agenda have institutionalised processes to make this happen. Several search firms have built specialisation in this space and HR teams have plans in place to address the constantly depleting middle management layer. However, organisations still need to make a start with making LGBT+ hiring mainstream. Unless we give it enough time and attention like we did to bringing women into the workforce, we will not get traction. After all, what gets measured, gets managed.
- Leadership commitment—Sounds cliche but it is the leaders who set the tone for this agenda to become top priority. Do leaders focus on one dimension (women) only? Do they fret because hiring diverse candidates is slowing down their plans? Leaders should become part of the talent acquisition solution rather than point fingers at talent acquisition teams for not bringing diverse candidates to the table. Equally, being patient when hiring targets are not met because someone is truly trying to build a diverse team, needs to become part of the organisation's DNA.
- Focus on the entire employee journey—While we have

not fully nailed down talent acquisition, it is important to think of the entire life cycle of the employee in the organisation. Do we talk about commitment to DEI and make abundantly clear the organisation's expectations from new joinees while onboarding them? Do we have robust policies against bad conduct such as bullying? Have we made our intent as an organisation visible by offering insurance policies that cover same-sex partners and gender affirmation surgery? Do we offer adoption leave? Do we spend time and resources on sensitising and training all employees on this and related subjects? Do we build programmes and provide platforms for employees to demonstrate their solidarity, support and allyship? The intent has to be to build a holistic approach to inclusion that is a reminder every step of the way in the employee's journey with the organisation.

I would like to share a quote that I came across a few years ago: *"Diversity is being invited to the party, inclusion is being asked to dance, belonging is dancing like no one is watching."* This has stuck with me as a wonderful way to think about the next step of the DEI journey. Let us all wholeheartedly belong, celebrate our unique differences and endeavour to make our communities the best they can potentially be!

Meetul Patel
Executive Director, Strategic Growth, Microsoft India

I was born in Zimbabwe, Africa, as part of the second generation from my family. I moved to the United States to study nuclear engineering. I followed this by an MBA from Wharton School of Business. After completing my education, I decided to work in the consulting field. Today, I have been a consultant for more than two decades.

My journey on LGBT+ (allyship) would have probably started about three decades ago, at college. At university in the US, this was something you had discussions on in the campus. But it was peripheral. It was not anything I was particularly passionate about or paying attention to.

Obviously, as you grow, your awareness on diversity and discrimination, and the fact that people need to be actively brought into the fold of society, and help through the groups, increases. I was born in an apartheid country. When I go all the way back to my history, I actually realise we had gone through that very discrimination on the basis of skin colour, more than anything else. As you get older, you begin to appreciate and understand what that was all about. That is when you also begin to see the patterns; how atypical communities and diverse groups are treated differently. I would like to add here, the active effort on allyship was truly on things that are obvious—race and gender.

equALLY

This is something I had at the top of my mind for the last two and a half decades, at least.

◆

Around 2009-2010, I came to India with plans to be here only for a year or two. Surprisingly, it has been over a decade now as there is a lot to do and contribute to here. India has just been a place where one year led to another, and that led to yet another and before you know it, it has been years.

There is an incredible number of things to do here and an incredible energy, for us to work with. I have been with Microsoft for the past 10 years and have run a number of their businesses here. Currently, I am working on strategic growth efforts focussed on helping the next billion, in terms of the adoption, leverage and use of technology.

About a few years ago, in a random conversation, an extremely fundamental question arose which perhaps hit on the LGBT+ community. We had been talking a lot about gender diversity, and not so much in India about ethnic diversity, frankly, but that would be another. And then all of a sudden, a question came up about, "Well, what about the LGBT+ community; about sexuality?"

I think that just made us hit the pause button to say, "Hang on a second. Why haven't we been thinking about this?"

I can not remember the specific meeting, but I know there was a time this came up and we said, "Hey, this is a community, it's sizeable and it's unheard. How come it's not an active thought process we all go through, to consider?"

While the Supreme Court always stated it is a miniscule minority, in reality the community is sizeable. Even if for the sake of argument, we accept it is a minority, then also the same principles would apply. However, given the significant size we were talking about, I was perplexed as to how come it was not so obvious, that we were engaged with it. Somewhere in that conversation, it hit me—"How come in a decade, I haven't had anyone who can really be open about this dimension of their life to me?" That somehow did not add up, because it is not possible in the thousands of interactions that I have had, I would not have had an open discussion about this point. That hit me!

Soon thereafter, an opportunity came up. A team member, Harsha and a few others in the organisation said, "It's time for us to create what we can call an Employee Resource Group (ERG). We've had this globally (in our global branches), why not in India?"

Although it is broadly a topic that was pretty active in terms of discussion in the broader global community in Microsoft, in India its absence was not something we could turn a blind eye to. Here was an opportunity for us, to take a more active role in helping this community and that led us to create this Employee Resource Group (ERG) which coordinates in Microsoft. And thus, the journey began, to at least start the process within Microsoft India.

Then of course, a big moment during that journey came when the Supreme Court rulings made it more obvious that there has been a point of discrimination which we need to address. The Supreme Court ruling raised the level of awareness everywhere. It kicked off the dialogue at a much higher volume, than it would have been at other places. There was a natural momentum, that kicked in, at least for our efforts in that process. But it is a journey.

I say this all the time. It is just the really early phase and it is going to take time. We have to move as quickly as possible to help people raise awareness, understand the issues and topics, provide, be prepared, be an ally in the appropriate way to the appropriate people. That will be the time. And then on, just keep that voice going.

I have always looked at 'Ally' as not being a noun, but fundamentally a verb; it's the kind where you have to act and grow over time.

◆

We are a society of incredible diversity, but sometimes it is not obvious or appreciated or present. When voices are few and possibly soft, when help and support is not apparent and available, allies play a significant role in helping bring the full spectrum of our communities forward.

Microsoft's mission of enabling every person and organisation on the planet to do more, compels us to understand everyone and be there to help. It drives us to appreciate the challenges and needs of all parts of society and to find ways to support everyone we can. It also drives us to include the talents and perspectives of all to help our communities and the world.

India just recently took a major step forward in its journey to bring equality to each of its citizens. A shift in laws is helping to gradually develop an environment that allows members of the LGBT+ community to be their authentic selves in everyday work and life. It has fostered a dialogue with the LGBT+ community and helped many develop a new understanding of its beautiful diversity. For those of us in the corporate world, it has provided the spark to develop a deeper understanding of our colleagues, face our conscious and unconscious biases, and extend our efforts to those whose differences may not be apparent.

Our ERG went through different levels before finally taking

the shape it is in today. Initially, it focussed on simple benefits and policies that we may have around health care, etc. Those were supportive and inclusive, which means there were adjustments made to that.

In the second level, we started with the basics like gender neutral washrooms and things like that to be facilitated. So, we began to inject that into the design criteria of buildings we were constructing.

The third is probably the most important one, which is actually the creation of an ERG and then figuring out its agenda, how it could begin a dialogue, the communication and awareness process. What this did was, it effectively created a constant voice throughout the entire Microsoft ecosystem, through updates you may give about the community, to events that you would sponsor, to a dialogue you may create with people from the community, to larger events and participation in pride rallies and things like that. So, all of that kicked off as a result of having this community.

It showed quick progress. We kept evolving, getting more active on the recruiting front, and participating in the right places to let people know, "We're open and we offer a more inclusive environment." This would make them feel fine about working with us.

Over the last few years, we have been on this journey to understand the community, and while we have a long way to go, we have developed a deeper understanding about the importance of allyship. Individuals are finding their personal manifestation of allyship. Some are quiet supporters, some show solidarity through engagements in events, some are active advocates and some are leaders shaping decisions to support the community.

My message to corporate leaders who are not an ally, or who are starting their journey to become an ally and to anyone who would want to start, would be simple—this is about being a good human being. It just starts with that fundamental notion of saying, "Am I allowing everybody to bring their full selves to whatever they do?" That is the anchor. And from that point, I think a series of questions will come in your mind naturally: "Have I heard everybody?" "Have I considered people from different communities?" "Am I encouraging or supporting inclusion?" "Am I being an ally or not?" Once you have the first foundation, the natural question will come up, "Who are the members of this community?" That could be followed by a curiosity about, "What concerns do they have?" or "What are the considerations we need?" And then, "How can I engage?" It will naturally flow.

For me, allyship means being a friend to those who seek it, and a voice to those who need it.

Allyship manifests itself in formal programs like the development of structured communities of allies, discussions for all to understand others more deeply, health benefits that consider the needs of the LGBT+ community, facilities that create comfort for all, or the proactive outreach to communities to join our team.

But most importantly, it manifests itself in the human acts of being friends and providing support. Allies speak up when others are not there to be heard or can not be or will not be. They are there to listen and understand and offer helping hands when needed. They are there to help bring everyone else's full selves forward.

I believe inherently that corporate leaders will be empathetic. So, I think if I had to summarise it—start with the fundamental foundation, that we all want to just be better human beings, and then tap into our empathy to help drive inclusion of everybody.

Mishkkaa Verma
Grade 9 Student
The Future Kid's School

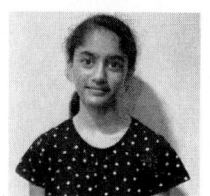

Let me start by asking you this question—How would you feel if someone constantly judged you, side-lined you and disrespected you for who you are? I bet you would not feel good about it. I bet that at one point you would start doubting yourself. Now, try imagining the lives of LGBT+ people who are struggling to be accepted by their families, relatives and friends for their sexual orientation. When one goes through these emotions, one needs someone to support them and confide into. In this scenario, the members of the LGBT+ community need more and more allies to come forward and support them. As fellow humans, it is our job to make everyone feel accepted and proud of themselves.

A lot of people wonder how to become an ally. I will try to give my perspective—it all begins with empathy. You do not have to be from the community to be an ally. You just need to support them. There are many ways in which you can be a good ally and show your support for the community. For example, sensitising people about the community, setting an example in the way you treat the members of the LGBT+ community, thereby inspiring others to do the same, standing up for those who are bullied for their sexual orientation and, last but not the least, grabbing all opportunities to create awareness, about the community, among people you know. Awareness and respect are the key qualities to being a true ally. If I want to make it simpler, I would say that being an ally simply means being a friend. Being an ally means we should do all that we would do for a friend.

Now, let me share a real-life story with you, of how my 79-year-old grandpa became an ally. My grandfather is a former Army officer and an anatomist. At first, he did not really understand the concept that people can have different sexual orientations. To him, sex and gender were the same thing. It took me a while to tell him that sex is the biological part of a being, but gender is a social construct. He was sceptical but curious, so after some time, he took the initiative and started watching videos, researching and reading articles about the LGBT+ community. This changed his point of view about the LGBT+ community in a positive way.

I am proud to say that today, even he is an ally. That brings me to the conclusion that if a 79-year-old man can change the way he thinks about the community, and can become an ally for them, then why can't we do it?

We all are like the pieces of a jigsaw puzzle, but the only way we will ever be able to see the bigger picture, is when we all unite.

Mohit Malhotra
MD and CEO,
Godrej Properties Ltd.

MY EXPERIENCE AS AN LGBT+ ALLY

Many years ago, I was driving around Mumbai when I saw graffiti on a nondescript wall of a broken building that read—"What will you be remembered for?". The more I thought about it, the more it made me think about my legacy, about my footprints in the sand. How will my children remember me? How will my organisation benefit from the decisions I make today? What impact will my actions have on society at large?

It is indeed a privilege to be leading a 2,000+ strong real estate organisation and be part of a group that is more than 125 years old. It is this position which empowers me to take decisions that have the potential to leave a lasting impact. Fortunately, I am supported by a team that shares my vision and enthusiasm to bring about long-term change through our policies and practices. The regular town halls, 'Be Live', hosted by me, also give me an opportunity to directly connect with all Godrejites at Godrej Properties Ltd (GPL) and drive long-term culture changes.

Today, I can proudly say that Godrej Properties is the only real estate organisation in India with gender diversity at almost 30%. It has not been an easy journey. But at GPL we have never shied away from a challenge worth taking. We have worked tirelessly to create a culture where members from the LGBT+ community feel not only safe and welcomed, but also encouraged to bring their whole selves to work.

From participating in job fairs to hiring candidates from the LGBT+ community, to actively leveraging our social media to reach out to a wide base within the LGBT+ community, we are doing it all. Our platform, Project Rainbow, under the Godrej Gig umbrella, aims to provide internships, contractual assignments and full-time opportunities to the community members.

Active focus on recruitment is also coupled with intense efforts to make our employees aware of their unconscious biases. Through regular workshops and conversations, we hope to further strengthen our inclusive culture.

We are still on this journey and are nowhere close to our destination, but I am glad that we have made a start and are progressing on our path with great gusto and determination.

Something that an out employee recently said, made me go back to that graffiti from many years ago, reassuring me that we are on the right track—"I feel so happy I don't have to hide who I am at work. My energy is not wasted in thinking what I can say and what I can't. This makes me more productive at work." This is the legacy everyone at GPL wishes to leave behind—a culture where we are respected and appreciated irrespective of our background, gender and sexual orientation.

Mohit Shukla

Managing Director, Head–India Legal and Lead–India Regulatory and Government Affairs, Barclays

Against the backdrop of Section 377 being on the statute book, Barclays began to explore whether it should introduce its global LGBT+ network, Spectrum, in India. There was a great degree of trepidation and nervousness about what that introduction would mean for colleagues in India. This was relevant given the experience at that time in a number of other Asian jurisdictions, where statute, social mores and other aspects influenced either caution or a more positive outlook.

As we debated the pros and cons, one of the questions was: When would be the right time to launch Spectrum in India? The response I had was that there never is, or would be, a right or a wrong time to introduce an initiative associated with something so intrinsically human. Fear distorts thought—Is this about a private act? Is this about a process of identifying and naming people? Is this token demonstration of support? Will we make ourselves or those we want to support, vulnerable? How wrong can it go?

As we grappled with these and many other views, as well as the legal position as the overlay, it became clearer that we should do this. We decided that Spectrum should be introduced in India.

Mohit Shukla

What does Spectrum represent? As an institution, Barclays unequivocally embraces diversity and inclusion, espousing a safe workplace. Spectrum, in its essence, is a voice and a force representing inclusion for a section of people which is, generally, unarguably, significantly excluded, for myriad reasons. Whether it is because LGBT+ people feel the need to hide, cannot speak for themselves, or cannot express themselves. The 'T' in the term, represents trans people who, more often than not, simply cannot step over the threshold. So, some are either in hiding or disguise, while the others are simply not out yet. Then how can any space claim to be safe or inclusive, unless a human being who looks and sounds different from the heterosexual norm can inhabit that space and find a confident voice, equally, in that norm?

We could discuss this, and many aspects of exclusion, which manifests in diverse ways in different spaces. I became an ally when I raised my hand to be the executive sponsor for Spectrum in India.

Since then, my wonderful colleagues have taken the network on an inspiring journey of awareness, and engagement with internal and external stakeholders, through dialogue, sensitisation and training. From creating gender-neutral washrooms, introducing medical insurance cover to support gender transition, to sourcing drinking water supply from a business enterprise that supports the transgender community, working with our vendors to encourage personnel from the community on our sites, engaging with a trans-persons resourcing partner, participating in diversity job-fairs, or engaging with India's first LGBT+ literary festival, or extending support to the first trans expedition to Mount Friendship, the endeavour underlying all of this is that someone can be themselves, entirely.

equALLY

We will not label, we will not name, we will celebrate every step that takes us further along the journey to inclusion at its broadest, as that should be the normal.

I thought I knew all about the community. Well mostly, when I began. However, as an ally, I have realised over the years that I know so little and have so much more to learn. Every step of the journey has revealed the rich, sometimes tragic, sometimes exhilarating, compelling layers and depths of this universe. I have come across inspiring personal stories of sadness, grit and perseverance; stories of achievement; epitomes of grace, dignity, brilliance. I have heard about people's experiences of raw human pain, sorrow and the hands clawing at the smooth impenetrable walls of exclusion, sometimes even breaking through them.

I admit that I have also learnt that the impatient surge for inclusion, vital and chafing as it is, needs, nevertheless, to deal with the journey, patiently. One could argue how much longer will it take, but as with any other human endeavour, one has to keep chipping away at it, bit by bit. And suddenly, one day, the wall of exclusion will give way. There will be no epiphany, and the world will never be perfect. But unless the community perseveres, and the allies are there on hand to stand behind it, support it visibly, vocally and meaningfully, an opportunity to make the world yet more equal, and the better for it, would be lost.

That is why I am, and will remain, a staunch ally.

Nandita Das
Actor and Filmmaker

FIRE AND ME

My journey of consciously understanding issues of the LGBT+ community began with *Fire* (1996), my first film as an actor. I literally stumbled upon it and I am glad that I did. It made me sensitive towards what we perceive as the 'other', which still remains a primary concern in much of my work. Thanks to *Fire*, I grew as a person. I say that not just because it exposed me to acting and films, but because of what I encountered after the screenings of *Fire*. I was appalled to see how insensitive and prejudiced our society is. I felt compelled to become a spokesperson for the issue, for people who were not being heard.

I grew up in a liberal home with an artist father and a writer mother. They were very inclusive and open. We discussed everything but, somehow, we never really spoke openly about homosexuality (at the time LGBT+ was not the term used, as there was not enough awareness about it). I shared the script with my mother and she put small chits of paper for the scenes which explored intimacy between the two characters. She was not sure how I would be able to do it. Initially, it was not easy. When I was asked to caress Shabana Azmi's face romantically, I must have done it unconvincingly. For I remember Deepa Mehta telling me, "Think of a man you love!" My reaction was,

"But she's not a man!"

It took me a while to go beyond my limited understanding of homosexuality, which was more intellectual than emotional. And there we were, three heterosexual women, making a film about a same-sex relationship! Soon, I got under the skin of the character, who was actually a lot like me—rebellious, impulsive and questioning. In fact, contrary to common perception, playing Sita has been easier than most of the characters I have played thereafter.

When the film came out, I was often asked if I was a lesbian. While I took it as a compliment for a performance that blurred the lines for the audience, I used to be quick to say, "No, I am not. You don't have to be a lesbian to play the part of a lesbian." But today, when I am asked the same question, I feel no need to be defensive. Instead, I ask, "Why is that question even relevant to the work I do? Maybe I am, maybe I am not!" Back then, even the savvy looking English journalists would struggle to use words like 'gay' and 'lesbian'. Instead, they would fumble and say, "That kind of a relationship!" Some rightly asked, "Why do you have to show two women in bad marriages for them to fall in love with each other?" Now, that is a very valid question. In retrospect, the only defence for this is that it provided the issue a gentler entry into the collective consciousness of a society that is uncomfortable with differing realities, prefers to have double standards, or prefers to be stuck in heteronormative stories.

Since *Fire* was my first film, people often asked me if I feared being stereotyped. But back then, I did not even know if there was going to be a second film, as acting was neither my dream, nor my ambition. So, I had no fear of it. Moreover, there have been so few films about same-sex relationships that there is no question about being type casted! I was hoping *Fire* would trigger more films which portray characters from the LGBT+ community in a sensitive manner, reflecting their reality. Sadly, one can literally count them on one's fingers.

We knew that *Fire* would be controversial and raise many eyebrows. Surprisingly, the censor board passed it without a single cut. I am not sure this would have happened today, as we have regressed in many ways. However, what we did not expect were violent reactions, that too after the film was in its third week of screening with 80 per cent collections. The initial reactions to *Fire* ranged from applauding it as a bold film to calling it dangerous, as some feared the film would turn all women into lesbians! And, of course, everything in between.

There were many failed attempts to ban *Fire*. In December 1998, theatres in Mumbai were bullied into cancelling shows. Some cinema halls were physically attacked, like the erstwhile Regal Cinema in Delhi. However, it was heartening to see that soon there were spontaneous protests comprising of people from all walks of life. They were questioning the self-appointed custodians of culture who were deciding for a whole country, what they should watch and what they should not. It became a larger battle for the right to free speech, expression and art.

While the fight continues, even after two decades, the discourse around the issue has significantly changed since then. There is still a lot more work that needs to be done to bring about greater awareness and eliminate discrimination. However, *Fire* started conversations and brought the issue out in the public domain like nothing else had before that, even though same-sex love was a crime back then.

In 2009, the Delhi High Court repealed the draconian Section 377 of the Indian Penal Code. We were thrilled about it. Though the legal battle culminated only on 6 September 2018,

equALLY

when the Supreme Court, in a landmark unanimous judgement, finally, decriminalised homosexuality. It was a memorable day as we now had a legal reform which had not seen the light of day for over 150 years! While this was a major victory, changing the mindset remains a challenge.

Unquestionably, *Fire* significantly impacted me, both—personally and professionally. And while I began to do more films after that, I always saw them more as a means to an end. My work on human rights issues and in films feed on each other, often blurring the lines. There are few films like *Fire*, which make such a profound impact.

Today, we live in a polarised world. There is an urgent need to fight discrimination at every level, be it gender, sexual orientation, religion, caste, colour or language. It is tragic that in our country it has become easier to hate, lynch, troll or put innocent people behind bars than it is to love whoever we want, freely.

Dr Nilakshi Roy
Associate Professor and
Head of Department–English,
Kerkar College

When my daughter Koninika came out to me, she was also grappling with her own journey. Like any other parent, I was not equipped to deal with it. To top it all, she was not very forthcoming about it. This pushed me further to question more.

It took me time to acknowledge that our lives will change in some ways for sure. Thankfully, I immediately brought this up with my counsellor. Fortunately, I had the right counsellor. She helped me clear away the cloud of doubt around Koninika's sexuality, whether this was 'normal' or not. My counsellor said that this feeling is absolutely okay and it is not going to change. Moreover, Koninika's sexuality really had nothing to do with her upbringing or any internal or external influence. That gave me a starting point. But it was not as easy as it appears in hindsight.

Now, when I reflect on that moment, I realise the critical role that the counsellor played in my journey of accepting my daughter's sexuality. I would really advise any parent to engage with the right counsellor—it is not very easy to find one, but not impossible. There are lists of queer-friendly counsellors available now.

I had extended family, both mine and my husband's, living

in the UK Apart from being doctors, they also had exposure to the LGBT+ community there. So, their credible advice and proactive support helped me a lot. Koninika's sister, who is three years older to her, also helped me with a number of blogs, articles and resources to educate myself about the community. I can say that I was lucky and blessed to find a lot of support from my family. After that, I remained in the orbit to continue my own journey of understanding and acceptance.

Accepting your child is one thing but becoming an ally or an advocate is another. Koninika invited me to attend the play 'Ek Madhav Baug' by Chetan Datar, and performed by actor Mona Ambegaonkar at the Humsafar Trust office. The play is a mother's journey to realising her son's sexuality and coming to terms with it. Of course, the play is very powerful and gripping, and leaves you with a lot to think about. However, it was the people of the community at the office, whom I remember more from the event. I felt like I was meeting my long-lost family. They were eagerly waiting to meet me and they spoke to me with such ease, as if I had known them forever! I knew I had found a new happy space. And I love inhabiting that space today. I count it as a privilege to know so many exceptional people in more ways than one!

I am often asked about how to become an ally and what one could do at a personal level or at a social level to become an ally. Well, at a personal level, you can do a number of small things to make a huge impact. By simply welcoming your child's choice to be different, applauding their inner strength—achieved after probably much hesitation or inner conflict—or by accepting their friends and their families from the community, you will create a huge difference in their life, as well as yours. In society, being an ally is about employing queer people, sharing unconditional bonds of support and friendship with them, supporting the causes of the community, speaking up when homophobic/transphobic comments are made and consciously avoiding/discouraging uninformed comments on issues facing the community. All of these are just suggestions. We all inhabit different spaces and go through different, unique journeys, so we can all find our unique ways to become an ally.

To all the parents, I would just like to say: Walk ten more steps than the extra miles your child has already crossed to be themselves. There is nothing to flaunt or hide. Cosmetics are mostly bad for health. There is one thing I always like to say, "I'm straight: Yes, about my daughter's queerness too!"

Nitya Bhalla
Data Science Leader and Diversity and
Inclusion Leader,
Nielsen South Asia

My journey as an active LGBT+ ally started when I witnessed my sister's child go through the journey of self-discovery from having self-doubts which sounded like, "Probably, I am gay!" to finally concluding: "I am actually a gorgeous lady".

At one point of time in this journey, my niece asked me if there was an opening in my company. While Nielsen has always been extremely open to everyone, I was not sure when it concerned the baby I had held in my hands since day zero. I felt there was still a lot to do before I could welcome her to work at Nielsen. So, when I was asked to be the Diversity and Inclusion (D&I) leader for Nielsen South Asia, I felt this was the right opportunity to make a difference. I luckily found a partner in my employee resource group (ERG) leader Aritra Kanjilal, who was also from the community.

Once I took the role, the first step was to build a passionate team willing to invest time and energy in this initiative. Next on the agenda was to expand the scope of what diversity and inclusion meant at Nielsen South Asia—from equal opportunities for women to a much broader canvas which would include multiple communities. At Nielsen, D&I is like a business initiative and like every investment requires a business case, this too needed one. The team prepared a business case which we presented to the leadership team. The global as well as the regional leadership team was extremely supportive, sponsoring us not just with money but also with active participation. This gave us wings. Imagine having your CEO as your CDO (Chief Diversity Officer)!

We started the journey by launching Pride ERG in Nielsen South Asia on Zero Discrimination Day 2019—our first PRIDE chapter in all of Asia with a video message from me to all the employees at Nielsen South Asia.

Post this, the team put on a full-fledged programme through the year to drive multiple initiatives across Nielsen offices. We had to start by building awareness and sensitising Nielsen members across all levels. We had our first pan-South Asia Pride Town Hall with speakers like Parmesh Shahani, Vice President and Head—Godrej India Culture Lab, Godrej Industries Ltd. and Associate Companies, and Zainab Patel, Director, Diversity and Inclusion, KPMG India on 17th May, 2019 to mark the 'International Day against Homophobia, Biphobia and Transphobia'. This in itself brought us close to 150 allies and the numbers have been growing since then, with many from the LGBT+ community sharing their personal stories internally as well as externally boosting awareness further, making sexual orientation, gender identity and expression, and sex characteristics more relatable for everyone.

From then on, there was no stopping us. We revised the insurance policies and even rephrased job postings. This also included revising our prevention of sexual harassment policy to make it more inclusive. We even went on to participate in the RISE Job Fair (India's first and biggest LGBT+ job fair) held by Pride Circle. We were at the Pride March in Mumbai and even shared our journey at the D&I Roundtable at Godrej. Currently, we are working on all-gender washrooms and all I can say is, the journey has only been satisfying. I would now feel comfortable to ask Saesha, my niece, to join Nielsen!

Nivruti Rai

Country Head, Intel India and Vice President, Data Platforms Group, Intel Corporation

I have been fascinated by numbers since I was a child and math was my favourite subject in school. I went on to do a B.Sc. in Statistics from Lucknow University and pursued an MS in electrical and industrial engineering from Oregon State University. When I got a job offer from Intel as a college graduate some 27 years ago, it was a dream come true. The rest, as they say, is history. Over the years, I grew as a technologist and a leader, going from design engineer to circuit technologist, principal engineer, senior director and, today, I serve as Country Head of Intel India and Vice President in Intel's Data Platforms Group.

I grew up in a small town in Uttar Pradesh, in a family with three daughters. Very early on, I learned about the biases people have against women. Eve teasing was common and, as a girl, I could not go out after dark for the sake of my own safety. Now that I have a young daughter, I really do not want her to see the world the way I have seen it.

I have had my share of obstacles as a woman in technology. From being one of only two women in an engineering batch of 70, to sometimes being the only woman in a conference room, I have felt the lack of gender diversity in the tech ecosystem and the negative perceptions that women are sometimes subjected to as a result. I recall once being mistaken for an administrative assistant because of my gender and the way I dressed. I never let that stop me from wearing what I wanted to. I realised that being true to myself and bringing my whole self to work gave me confidence.

My first exposure to the LGBT+ community was when I was in school. I was a big fan of Boy George, a talented singer with a penchant for androgynous fashion. So, I became aware of different gender identities and sexual orientations when I was fairly young. I never thought anything of it because children are accepting by nature. I think bias is something people learn as they grow up and, as adults, they become set in their ways.

It was sometime during my early career that I started to learn more about the LGBT+ community and wanted to become an ally. A close colleague of mine broke down in tears one day at work and when I tried to console her, she told me that it was about her son. At first, I thought he may have been diagnosed with a terminal illness, but it turned out that he had come out as gay. My reaction was one of relief and over the next few days I tried to help her to move towards acceptance. And in counselling her, I learned a lot myself. It has been many years since then and I am sure things have improved a great deal, but we still have a long way to go.

Another story that stands out in my memory is one that my driver told me, about a transgender person in his village who was beaten to within an inch of their life, for no reason other than their gender. While this was a hate crime which all of us can recognise for its brutality, we should realise that bias is just as prevalent among the educated and the privileged. It just manifests in different ways.

As an ally, I have never received a negative reaction or been questioned for showing my support for the LGBT+ community.

I am aware that this is a luxury afforded to me by virtue of my position, so I take it as an opportunity to speak up and have my voice heard.

Recently, I went out of my way to help someone who was struggling because his family did not accept him. His life was becoming very hard here in India and, ultimately, I helped him relocate to the US. I do not like to see people hurting just because of who they are. You can not be happy if you can not be yourself and if people are not happy, they will not be good workers, good family members or friends.

I think anyone can become an ally as long as they believe that hate is learned and can be unlearned. All of us are at some point along this journey of unlearning our biases and learning to embrace our differences. Having a finger pointed at you for being different always hurts, but remember, those who try to hurt you are the ignorant ones. I believe we should celebrate our differences because that is what makes us unique. Diversity of backgrounds, experiences, of thought and understanding, has great value and that is what drives innovation.

To the LGBT+ community, and to anyone who is diverse or different in any way, I say, find your allies. If you think of the world as a normal distribution in probability theory, you will find that there are always people willing to support you. Find people who accept you, respect you and appreciate you for who you are.

Let me leave you with Derek Sivers' first follower principle: "It's hard for the first person who dares to stand out from the crowd, and it takes courage for the second person to join in, but it only gets easier as others join them and transform it into a movement."

Pankajam Sridevi
Managing Director (India),
Commonwealth Bank of Australia

I do not think I was an ally from the beginning. In fact, I think I was biased and very obstinate to the idea of accepting the LGBT+ community. From 2008, I remember engaging a lot with my colleagues in New Zealand and Australia. When my managing director recommended Bruce (name changed) for an expat role in India, I was very excited because Bruce was really good and I was certain he would deliver the role very well. However, when the business leader informed me that Bruce is gay, I started having inhibitions. While on the face of it I made it appear that I was okay with it, I started giving irrational excuses to the business leader on how Bruce will not fit in Indian society and the team here will not accept him. I now realise that I was blocking a fabulous and talented professional to come into my team because of my own inhibitions.

Things changed when more of my friends came out to me. When someone I knew came out to me it helped me change my perspective. A close friend of mine from Melbourne was in Bengaluru and I took him out for dinner. As I started talking about my family, showing him pictures of them, he responded by showing pictures of his family, "This is my partner". I was not expecting a male person, so I almost fell off my chair! For me, it was only the two opposite genders—female and male—that could be together. I composed myself and continued the conversation. My friend later told me that he had purposefully introduced his partner to me since he wanted to be true to me and also make sure that his personal choices are not disrespectful for our friendship. I was really moved by this gesture and I started to be inclusive in my mind. I am indeed thankful to him for this.

The major push, however, was during a business discussion with an ex-colleague. We had organised a video call and once the business discussions ended, we decided to just chit-chat about each other's lives. After exchanging light-hearted formalities, she started to open up and told me how she had recently got to know about her son identifying as a transgender. For some reason, it didn't surprise me and I was exceptionally calm. I appreciated the trust and confidence she had shown in me by sharing this. We talked more about how it helps children if parents become allies first. Being a mother, I could empathise with her. Sometime during that chat, my mind, soul and heart had taken another leap towards acceptance and inclusivity.

I was floored when I noticed a 57-year-old mother advertising for a groom for her son, Harish Iyer. They lived in Mumbai. I could not believe my eyes! A brahmin woman accepting that her son is gay? Unbelievable! After a few seconds, I could understand her mind. She was breaking the barriers that we, as humans, had set for ourselves, through the love for her son. She had not only set a benchmark for others but also opened the eyes of many, including me. This particularly struck a chord with me and I was galvanised to do something.

It occurred to me that I was leading an organisation that had thousands of employees from all parts of India. I had heard accounts from women and persons with disabilities about their struggles in finding jobs even when they have equal qualifications as others. This made me think about the LGBT+ community members who were also facing massive stigma both at their home and workplace. I started to wonder as to how many of my team members were closeted and were unable to share their core identity.

I thought to myself, how as a part of an international organisation, I am very distinct in my dressing style. I only wear a saree, apply a big 'bindi' on my forehead with vermillion too. It is very easy to identify that I am a married Indian woman. Now imagine if I was asked to 'hide' my identity just because I was different and that some groups would not accept it. I would get stressed, feel unhappy and would almost perish in that environment. To top it all, this would have affected my potential immensely. I realised there could be many team members who would be in an uncomfortable situation and would benefit if I came out strongly to support the cause.

In a very short time, we formed the Pride Network. This was at the time when Section 377 was still prevalent in India and many leaders were not comfortable to openly become an ally. I stood in a crowded room and said emphatically, "I respect the sexual orientation of every person and fully support them as they are. As a group we will treat them with respect and equality." It created a huge impact on me as I declared myself as an ally.

I am determined to continue bringing in the LGBT+ community members to work with me and my team and create an atmosphere of friendship and respect. I realise the only way to get more allies is to talk about the impact of inclusion to our colleagues and family, and lead, from the front on the change. This quote sums it all—"All people are equal; it is only virtue that differentiates them."

Pavan Vaish
Head of Driver and Supply Operations,
Uber India and South Asia

IN WHAT WAYS CAN ONE BE AN ALLY TO THE LGBT+ COMMUNITY

Organisations across the world are going through a diversity and inclusion (D&I) revolution. The most progressive organisations today, have targets to incorporate policies and initiatives promoting D&I. This is no longer an HR mandate, but a part of the overall business strategy. I have been extremely lucky to be a part of inclusive organisations which not only recognise but also work towards empowering diverse communities.

In order to be an ally to the LGBT+ community, I believe you need to constantly challenge assumptions on gender, orientation and identity. You need to speak up when you witness unsupportive behaviour. That is when you go from being a supportive bystander to an ally. When people around you see you as a vocal and visible ally, they too want to do their bit in uplifting the LGBT+ community that has been underrepresented for so long.

Unfortunately, the social fabric we live in does not allow individuals to be free, but we are getting there, especially in modern workplaces. The key to unleashing your true potential, personally and professionally, is to be emotionally centred and be at peace with yourself. I understand this might be easier said than done, so my advice would be to build a community of friends and family who enable you to be your true self.

I strongly believe in mentorship, where leaders from the LGBT+ community can help guide individuals entering the workforce. Studies have shown that despite expanding training and D&I programmes, organisations struggle to see results with improved equality and diversity in the workplace. By involving senior leaders and increasing the on-the-job contact with females, LGBT+ individuals and historically underrepresented workers, organisations can promote social accountability from the top down.

In organisations especially, opening the door for underrepresented people is not enough. We need to address the factors which prevent so many of them from walking through it. More importantly, succeeding once they're inside, by de-biasing systems and removing the barriers encountered by diverse talent, both before and after the hiring process. Organisations and employees need to take charge and drive the change. At Uber, we have employee resource groups (ERGs) that ensure equal representation of the needs of all employees including promoting LGBT+ inclusion and diversity.

Another important aspect of being a good ally includes acknowledging your own privilege and bias to create empathy. It is important to focus on not just supporting the community but actively driving awareness around the challenges that the LGBT+ community faces. It is our responsibility as leaders to understand, internalise and guide each other to move forward and create a diverse and inclusive workplace for everyone.

At Uber, we believe by encouraging employees to bring their authentic selves to work we can build the highest performing diverse workforce in the industry. We have established a Diversity Advisory Council which now functions as an advisory body to help us implement diversity, equity, inclusion, and belonging initiatives. We continue to review, redesign and embed an inclusive mindset into our systems and programmes to help employees thrive and succeed. We have also institutionalised Gender Transition Guidelines for transgender, non-binary and gender non-conforming employees who are planning, or going through, a gender transition. These guidelines not only help employees but also encourage their families and friends to be more supportive through the transition process.

Organisations in this day and age need to realise that in order to attract top talent, they need to not only reinvent themselves, but also prioritise an inclusive and diverse culture, which should go hand in hand with the company's vision and business priorities. An easy way for GenZ to identify these companies is to look out for those that include sexual orientation and gender identity in their non-discrimination policies, along with companies that have made a public commitment to hiring more LGBT+ employees. Companies which are purpose driven with a strong sense of accountability and corporate social responsibility are also predisposed to policies promoting equality in the workplace, often acting as agents of social change.

Payal Pasha
Parent, Poetess,
Animal Activist and Homemaker

At the time of our wedding, my husband Javed Akhtar Pasha had three daughters. Though I had not met the children before, his family members had told me that since the beginning, the eldest daughter (six years old at the time) always behaved like a boy. Her choice of clothes and toys, and conduct were of a boy rather than that of a girl. And I observed the same. She preferred outdoor sports and had the same aggression and energy that boys usually have when growing up. No one around her, not even her friends, knew that she was not a boy biologically. We all believed her to be a 'tomboy' and that this was a phase which would eventually pass as she grew up.

She was living with her aunt until high school. It was only when she moved in with me that I was able to observe her closely. She was always secretive and bottled things up. One day I noticed her crying in her room after she had returned from school. I went up to her and coaxed her to share what she was feeling. She was, of course, hesitant, but then she told me that some boys had teased her at school as "the boy with breasts", while playing basketball. She said, "I am a boy. I am not a girl." I realised something needed to be done about the situation. That is when Aryan's journey began.

I went to my husband and explained the situation. He was

slightly taken aback and not fully convinced with my idea of a physical transformation for the child. He initially thought I wasn't serious. It took a bit of discussion to explain that his daughter would always remain frustrated if we do not help her complete the journey of becoming the boy that she believes she is. My husband eventually agreed to it and said he was on board if that would make her happy. It also helped that almost everyone already thought of her as a boy and she was always treated like one in the family. So, it was not that challenging to have our family on board—not just for the gender affirmation surgery but also for announcing it in public.

I did not know much about the LGBT+ community then. I probably knew a bit about being gay or lesbian, but not transmen. I do not think I ever saw it from the lens of Aryan being a part of the community. The only thing I saw was my child's happiness and how I needed to support him to make it happen. After Aryan's transformation, I got to know the community up close.

Being open about Aryan being a transman, brought a lot of opinions and biases my way. However, I remained firm. I tried to bust the myths and misinformation people had and kept it clear that this is my child—my son, this is my opinion and I believe in it. I did not care much for the opinions of others.

Family is the first school of life for any child. The foremost thing any parent must do is to be cognizant of the fact that their child is an LGBT+ person, embrace it gracefully and proceed to educate themselves along with their child about the community in all its aspects. In case any physical transformation is needed, holding the child's hand through the difficult journey of transition will make them take the leap of faith. When faced with adversity, ridicule and sometimes hatred, it is the parents' love and strength that can help the child sail through. A kiss, a hug, a smile and not caring much about "what will people say", make for an ironclad armour that every LBGT+ kid needs, to be able to stand upright with pride.

I want to reinforce that your child is 'normal'. They are not a special kid with special needs. Treat them with the same dignity with which you would treat any other member of your family. Your child is not a circus clown. Do not go around announcing their 'condition' to satisfy your sense of modernism. Do not be ashamed and avoid talking about your child's journey through life. Instead, stand tall and proud while sharing their success stories with people who really matter. Do not judge their capability to handle even the most difficult situations in life. Just be there always. That is enough.

Ramkumar Narayanan
VP Technology and Managing Director, VMware India

Diversity and inclusion (D&I) at the workplace is a topic that is being discussed more than ever before and with good reason. While it once may have seemed like a catchphrase, today, all leading organisations agree that when each employee brings their own brand of thought and experiences to the table, it creates a more innovative, positive environment and a broader, global perspective. The bottom line? A stronger environment and a more profitable company. D&I initiatives are not just tools or platforms designed to uplift or enable a stronger workforce, but key drivers that empower talent, increase collaboration and accelerate innovation to improve the bottom line. I believe that by harnessing the power of human difference we can build a community that is inclusive and diverse, thus creating a rich tapestry of collective experience.

For long, the LGBT+ community has grappled with several issues not excluding social acceptance and associated stigma. Unfortunately, the challenges are not limited to the workplace, but indicate a larger societal issue. However, this is slowly changing course and I am happy to see a shift in the right direction with progressive organisations leading the way and more often than not, setting an example. It is heartening to see transformative changes that are deeply aided by actions.

Creativity is amplified by diversity, and it is a win-win even from a business perspective.

The big picture is to create a workplace/society/community where everyone can feel a sense of belonging each and every day, and is empowered to stand up and lead.

My personal and professional journeys have both been shaped by an environment of acceptance—of people from different cultures, faiths and social beliefs. At its core, my journey has been about the upliftment of society. My formative professional years in the US and then in India, strengthened my belief that strong results can only be achieved by harnessing the opinions of people, however different they are from one's own. Healthy debate and an empowered workforce are my operating mantras.

The word 'ally' is a recent addition to my vocabulary. However, my first introduction to the LGBT+ community was in the late 1980s, as a student and a young professional in the US. The 1980s were a different time when conversations around homosexuality had just started to gain traction, but not always in a positive light. The one incident that stood out to me was when I was a graduate student. A project teammate featured in our campus newspaper as an LGBT+ activist. While it did not change the focus and dynamics within our workgroup, there were a variety of reactions from others in the class.

In my first exposure to the community, I learned that societal acceptance greatly varied depending on one's personal beliefs and views. For the person involved, it requires a lot of courage and support from their family and friends.

The second incident came a few years later when a mid-level manager at a company I was employed with, at the time went through gender reassignment. The reactions were alarming. I noticed a sudden change in the behaviour of co-workers who until then were regularly interacting with this person at work and outside of it. The organisation's lack of preparedness to deal with the situation and to extend support to the individual was clear. There was no gender agnostic restroom for the person as neither male nor female colleagues felt comfortable sharing the space with the individual. The experience must have been so distressing for the person. That said, I am glad to see a drastic change in the acceptance of the community today. Granted, we are not fully there yet, but I believe that our society has come a long way over the past 20 years.

In all the organisations that I have worked with so far, I am very proud of the efforts VMware has been making to address and remedy the challenges faced by the LGBT+ community. While the global D&I team has been making a concerted effort, our D&I team in India, for which I am the local executive sponsor, has been making great strides in furthering the local efforts that are nuanced for the country. A few such examples would be, a homegrown group of actors in the organisation, that use theatre as an educational instrument to broach difficult topics and allow for safe conversations; displaying pronouns in written communication; celebrating the month of Pride with a 21-day allyship programme to grow the number of allies and provide greater awareness around Pride. As I work with our teams and the larger community, I continue to learn more about the community and how we can serve it better as an ally.

My first message to those who are not an ally yet or who are just starting their journey, would be to take the time to walk in the shoes of people from the Pride community. Learn about their aspirations and everyday challenges, be aware and more accepting; pledge to support equality for all persons.

Also, incorporate inclusivity in the way you think, speak,

behave and conduct business. Treat everyone with respect and acknowledge the value they bring to the table at the workplace and outside of it.

Finally, talk to those who are ahead of you in the journey to understand how they were able to overcome bias, stereotyping, and extend their support to the community. Consider these points before forming your own strategy about how to become an informed ally.

Sanjay Murdeshwar
Country President and Managing Director, Novartis India

AN ALLY OR AN INDIVIDUAL WHO RESPECTS A FELLOW HUMAN BEING?

When I first decided to pen my thoughts around whether I am an ally, it led to an interesting introspection which I am sharing here. I asked myself, "Have I represented those who know the words, but have no voice? Have I participated in any Pride Parade or fought for an LGBT+ cause?" To be honest, the answer is 'No'. Yet, I believe I am an ally because my core belief informs me that every individual has the right to pursue their happiness and must be celebrated.

Truth be told, growing up in Mumbai in a cocooned environment, I was more exposed to the concept of 'difference' than 'diversity'. My knowledge and ecosystem were restricted. Neither in my family and friends circle, nor in my school or community was I introduced to different sexual orientations—lesbian, gay, bisexual, etc. So, I was unaware and had no inherent opinions. If you are unaware about something, how can you form an opinion about it? I must admit that being unaware was possibly a blessing in disguise. My parents never imposed their personal views on me. Being 'a good person' was the only virtue celebrated at home. This helped me build my views with an unbiased mindset and shaped my core belief.

Of course, the risk in being ignorant is that, one is not consciously supporting a fellow human in their choices. So in hindsight, my first lesson was that, being aware makes one look at issues and individuals in a rational manner.

My journey led me to live across the world: Germany, Singapore, the US and the Philippines, besides India. Further, my passion for travel enabled me to explore cultures, histories and socio-economic systems. Most importantly, it pushed me to meet and accept people from diverse backgrounds along with their unique individualities. This was absolutely educative. It introduced me to various experiences and thoughts, which further evolved my understanding of individuals and society on the whole. My second lesson was that the more one experiences, the more one learns to celebrate and appreciate diversity, and its advantages to both, individuals and society.

This prompts me to share a personal story. A very close friend of mine, someone I have known for a long time, who is as good as family to me, came out publicly. We had celebrated festivals and even vacationed together, but he never indicated or even shared that he was gay. Perhaps, he was also coming to terms with it. Initially, I was surprised. Later, it dawned on me that perhaps he did not come out even to me due to the challenges and stigma around coming out along with the fear of prejudice and non-acceptance. Our society is still learning to accept, respect and treat all as equals. This made me more conscious and I vowed to be a vocal ally. Here, I would like to share my third lesson: Make a conscious effort to drive an environment of inclusivity. Do not remain a bystander.

While family and friends play a very important role in providing the much-needed support, an inclusive workplace helps in building confidence and instils a feeling of equality among all genders.

I am proud to be at Novartis, where we are continuously striving to create a safe and inclusive workplace that supports diverse gender identities. We believe that everyone should be free to be their best and true self at work, without the fear of discrimination. That is why, we support the UN Standards of Conduct for Business, tackling discrimination against LGBT+ people. We have also been recognised by the Thomson Reuters Global Diversity and Inclusion Index as one of the world's most diverse companies.*

We actively promote LGBT+ equity and awareness to improve the lives of our colleagues and shape positive societal impact. Recently, we extended the definition of family to include same-sex partners and amended our policies. Our health insurance now covers families including same-sex partners and their children, along with gender reaffirmation surgery costs. We have also enhanced our hiring efforts through onboarding of specialised recruitment partners who connect us with the LGBT+ community. All of these initiatives, and many more, are constantly evolving at Novartis. When each of us feels included, we can contribute more, and we all benefit.

In conclusion, my message is that both in our professional and personal capacity, we must be proactive and work towards protecting, respecting and valuing a person's individuality regardless of their gender or sexual orientation, as every individual deserves to blossom.

---

*The Diversity & Inclusion Index launched by Thomson Reuters, annually ranks 100 organisations as the most diverse & inclusive workplaces globally.

Saptorsi Hore
Head of Operations,
ThoughtWorks, India

I was not familiar with the term, 'LGBT+ ally' until a few years ago, when I was introduced to it at a sensitisation and awareness workshop in 2017. I was encouraged to reflect upon some of my experiences up to that point in life. As I did that, a big realisation hit me. I knew next to nothing about LGBT+ issues and the experiences of people who belonged to that community in India. I reflected on why I had not been inquisitive about LGBT+ issues in the first place, despite having met a person in the year 2000 who identified as part of this community.

I travelled to Phoenix, US in the year 2000, for a client project. This was my first trip outside India. As expected, it took me a few days to adjust to a new place, time zone, culture and work environment. As I settled in, I realised I was not completely at ease, especially, around one particular team member, Alex. He seemed markedly different and I could not put my finger on why I felt guarded around him. Cathy, the project lead at the time, sensed my awkwardness and brought it up, during a one-on-one conversation with me. I was mortified at being called out, but Cathy's candour and empathy quickly put me at ease. She realised that I had not met anyone, until this project, who was an out and proud gay man. She suggested I do some self-learning, understand more on LGBT+ and inclusion in our workplace. She suggested that I should begin engaging with Alex and be more inclusive in my behaviour.

Reading about USA's LGBT+ community was eye-opening, as I learnt about the discrimination faced by people belonging to the community. However, it was not as easy as a switch being turned on or off. It took me a few days to become comfortable around Alex. Informal settings like team lunches and bowling games helped me get to know him better. I was able to see that he was as entitled as anyone else to express himself through his choice of mannerisms, speech, expressions and attire. Alex recognised the change in me and reciprocated with greater authenticity and freedom in our interactions. Finally, we both felt safe with each other. Eventually, I returned to India after three months and moved onto another project.

It took a few weeks for a new project, team and deliverables to take centre stage, and I relegated my experience in Phoenix to the back of my mind.

ThoughtWorks India has always focussed on diversity and inclusion (D&I) at the workplace. This helped me restart my journey of learning about the LGBT+ community, specific to the Indian context and our workplace here.

One of my significant lessons was that allyship is diverse. The spectrum of LGBT+ allyship ranges from public expressions of support, to expressing oneself through individual acts. However, all aspects of allyship are important. This valuable lesson gave me the confidence to arrive at an approach that worked for me as an ally. My personality, allows me to be most comfortable in expressing support and inclusivity through my language, using verbal and non-verbal cues.

This self-awareness was a journey in itself. It involved

attending sensitisation workshops, being actively involved in the hiring of LGBT+ people at ThoughtWorks and conducting the 'Being Inclusive—Unconscious Bias' workshops for other ThoughtWorkers. I also participated in activities of the Mitra Collective - ThoughtWorks India Affinity group for the LGBT+ and allies community. This collective works towards building a safe and inclusive workspace. It also drives initiatives externally through various partnerships and programmes. As part of the leadership team, I have supported and encouraged our internal programmes like 'Interning with PRIDE' — an internship programme, specifically designed for the LGBT+ community, to support their journey in the domain of technology. As always, policies play a key role in building an inclusive and a safe workplace. So I have ensured that we have the right policies. Some LGBT+, specific policies include the 'Gender Affirmation and Transition at the Workplace policy', for our transgender employees; and medical insurance that covers same-sex partners. We are actively on the look out to customise our policies to support everyone's needs.

"In my experience of working with different companies, I have made an important observation—it is only when one brings their authentic self to work that they truly experience personal and professional growth. Organisations should proactively foster a culture of inclusion and belonging by supporting people in their personal journeys. This is especially important to the GenZ LGBT+ community, who are beginning their career and want to join companies that champion a progressive and equitable culture. A place where 'we' and 'us' prevail over 'I' and 'me'."

While there is still a long way to go, I do feel a sense of pride in the vibrant and inclusive community that ThoughtWorks India has nurtured. I feel a sense of belonging in this environment where anyone can bring their whole and authentic selves to work. I look forward to more people from the LGBT+

community choosing to be a part of ThoughtWorks, and us being an employer of choice for all. I know this will help both, ThoughtWorks and me, on our journey of inclusion and allyship.

Shaina Shingari
Breaking Barriers Campaigner,
Kick Start Equality Campaigner and
Special Olympics Bharat Campaigner

My name is Shaina Shingari and I study in Grade 9 at Tagore International School, Vasant Vihar. I am interested in sports, nature photography, sketching and playing the piano. I am fortunate to be born into a literate family. Respect for everyone in society, irrespective of their religion, wealth, caste, colour, etc., and believing in equal rights, has been a part of my upbringing. The seeds of empathy, caring and compassion were sown in me right from an early age. And I am proud of the fact that I am receiving the same training in my school as well.

Apart from academics and gaining knowledge in school, I have joined various student-led campaigns that require my equal attention. These include the Breaking Barriers campaign, which aims at sensitising schools about human rights; the Kick Start Equality campaign, which spreads awareness about gender inequality; and the Special Olympics Bharat, which works towards the inclusion of people with mental or physical disabilities in society.

I believe that it is important to not only earn the respect of others, but more importantly, show them respect. This, I believe, is the foundation of meaningful relationships and, therefore, of leadership. I also believe that if we inspire a group of people to believe in something, we can motivate them towards positive transformation. Furthermore, I believe when we take out time to invest in others, they will return great value. Which means that when we invest in other people, we are investing in the future of our country.

My allyship with the LGBT+ community started with the Breaking Barriers campaign at school. It is a purely student-led, sustainable campaign that helps in understanding and spreading awareness about sexuality and human rights which started in 2013, with the aim of sensitising the youth, especially school students, about human rights. As part of the campaign, members conduct gender sensitisation sessions in schools and colleges across the city to spread awareness about gender equality, bullying and discrimination in schools. I would urge more schools to follow our footprints to make their campus an inclusive space for all by believing and exercising human rights.

I joined the campaign when I stepped into the ninth standard. Being a newcomer in the school, I was not aware about the collaborations and partners of the campaign. In June 2020, the school project director informed me about its collaboration with Pride Circle. She inspired the members to participate in the #21DaysAllyChallenge. This challenge gave me the opportunity to take a stand and use it as a platform to spread awareness about the LGBT+ community, especially in terms of the hardships they go through in order to normalise their identity. I decided to do my utmost to get them the support and the respect they deserve. I started to read more about the community, watched documentaries and shared the knowledge I had gained about the community with friends and family through conversations.

My allyship with the community has instilled self-esteem and confidence me. So there are no such awkward moments when someone is unhappy with my decisions. The other members are highly supportive. The only struggle is to balance academics with the demands of the campaign.

I chose to spread awareness among the youth instead of elders due to the insight that I gained while working for this campaign. I learned that today's youth is far more knowledgeable and advanced to understand the need to do away with the discrimination of fellow humans that we come across each day. I believe that we, the young students, can together bring a positive change in society and create a safe world for everyone by spreading awareness on equal rights, respecting everyone and treating everyone in a fair and just manner. Let us, together, believe in equity more than equality.

Simar Singh
Managing Director, Group Operations,
Hyderabad, UBS India

As an individual, I thrive in chaos as I am able to create structures in it. By nature, I am perpetually curious. I enjoy gathering experiences and being driven by the new. I am extremely passionate about diversity, in terms of gender, as well as experiences and ideas. Unfortunately, the way corporate structures are defined, the diverse dots never get connected. Even when people hire, they end up hiring someone exactly like themselves. I enjoy connecting diverse thoughts because when you connect these dots, the potential is limitless.

I am married and have two kids. Both are boys—the elder one is 17, the younger one is 12. Over the past 15 years, we have moved across five different countries together, and the boys have always been super excited about change. I think they have learnt to manage the chaos I create in their life.

During my tenure at HSBC, I played the two critical roles—run the bank or change the bank.[*]

---

[*] 'Run the bank' typically refers to day-to-day activities required to support the ongoing activity within a bank. 'Change the bank' refers to an activity aimed at improving how the bank operates, including enhancements to IT, Operations, Customer Service, Sales and Marketing and other areas.

equALLY

Working with managers or team members from the LGBT+ community had helped me become more aware. However, on a scale of 10, maybe I was at 1 or 2. I was transferred to Bengaluru in 2018, to manage the Global Service Center Bangalore. In this role, I was looking at driving collaboration and change.

One of my first few meetings in Bengaluru was with our diversity and inclusion (D&I) champion, Gunveen Ahuja, who shed light on the work happening on inclusion at the office. She asked me if I was supportive of driving the agenda for Pride, and introduced Pride Circle as an organisation which does a lot of work on the same.

"I think we should engage with them," she suggested.

"Yes, absolutely! Let's participate and get connected," I said.

All this while I was thinking of building 'Pride' in the HSBC brand. This was how 'unaware', I was. By the end of the conversation, Gunveen realised I was lost. So, she wanted to know if I was aware of what we were talking about, and in typical corporate bluff I said, "Obviously!"

That evening, on the way to airport, I was stuck in the famous Bengaluru traffic for a while. That is when I looked up Pride Circle on Google and did some basic research on Pride, to gain context around the conversation I had had earlier. Like everyone else, my first reaction was, "Is it such a big problem? I am sure we are making a big fuss about nothing."

That led me to join the Pride Circle group on WhatsApp, as a fly on the wall. I read the conversations happening under the Bangalore Pride group. And frankly, that week was an eye-opener. Just by following the conversations, I could understand the unconscious biases we harboured at work. In fact, these biases were everywhere. Every event and activity has its biases, hidden in plain sight across the organisation.

Through this group I got to hear a few personal stories, of how people from the LGBT+ community have had to live their entire life closeted. It is made worse when society begins to enforce so-called 'corrective action' on them.

Later, I called Gunveen and told her that I now understood what she was talking about, and that she had my complete support. Sometime in September 2018, we launched the employee resource group (ERG) for Pride in Bengaluru. We started by taking baby steps. A couple of days later, I saw the HSBC Rainbow Lion mug. While I was very sceptical of the change these mugs were driving, like usual corporate gimmicks around building visibility, they had to be done.

That week I took one of these Rainbow Pride mugs home. My in-laws were visiting us at that time. I kept the mug on the table calling it an HSBC goodie. It looked nice and colourful. After a while, I asked a question: "Do you know why this is in rainbow colours?" Nobody on that table had a clue. I briefly touched upon the topic only to be immediately interrupted by my mother-in-law. She brushed the conversation under the carpet, asking me to stop, as the kids were around!

Though it seemed that the incident was meant to be forgotten—it was not. A few days later, while thinking about this incident, I realised that we need to start this conversation (Pride sensitisation) at home, for the change to be sustainable. Conversations confined to work will not solve the issue. We need to start making that change in the community as a whole!

◆

The challenges with Pride are manifold. It is so pervasive and deeply ingrained in us. Unless we give them airtime, discuss them, the challenges will continue to feed on our collective ignorance. It will continue to remain something that is discussed in whispers, and people will continue be scared of addressing it! Due to their ignorance, a large part of the world believes there is no problem around the LGBT+ community. Meanwhile, others are scared about what the world will say: "Will I be considered a part of the LGBT+ community if I show solidarity?"

We started running events at HSBC India called Amplifying Pride events which were basically half-day events hosted in the office with participation from industry leaders, and other ERG leads in the city. The idea was to take everyone on a journey and start collaborations by sharing learnings. The world is made up of communities and it is people from these communities who come into the workplace. So, we need to think about sustainable change. It must become a part of life. I used to wear a Pride pin and a Pride lanyard to make a visible commitment towards being an LGBT+ ally. Generating employment is another big lever for D&I and hence participating in RISE—the job fairs helped achieve this.

We started using LinkedIn and other social media channels, to share our journey widely. In fact, many of my LinkedIn posts on these topics had 25,000+ reach, and high engagement.

One of the highlights at HSBC in 2019 was the Pride walks in which employees carried a 90-m long Pride flag which went across all the cities where we operate out of—Hyderabad, Bengaluru, Kolkata, Vizag, Chennai, Pune—increasing awareness, and pulling people out of their shells. And in 2020, we got HSBC to participate in the #21DaysAllyChallenge, and it ended up being in the top 5!

Slowly, over the past two years, there have been multiple interventions for us to be able to bring this conversation home. It is a big challenge because while we do a lot of things in the organisation, the moment we go home, we forget all about them and do not want to talk about it. However, the fact is that people live in communities and we need to be talking about it there too. This conversation has to be much bigger and it has to be consistent across homes and corporates.

There were some uncomfortable conversations with my conservative Big Fat Punjabi Family, from sharing a Pride-themed kids' story book for my 5-year-old niece, to having more dinner table conversations with my 75-year-old father, but today the entire family is more aware.

I still remember the day when one of my cousins saw my LinkedIn post about the Pride ERG and called me to say, "I'm impressed, Big Bro, seeing the way you are publicly speaking up for the community." That boosted my confidence and built faith in me that there is surely hope for my attempts to create awareness.

There is a strong need for allyship. We must encourage everyone to increase their awareness. The responsibility is for each and every one of us to make the LGBT+ community's struggles visible. There is something that everyone can do. The first thing is to get educated on the issue, and then become a part of the conversation. Even the smallest action goes a really long way. I joined UBS this year where I continue my journey of allyship.

Sindhu Gangadharan
SVP and MD,
SAP Labs India

As humans, we take pride in being the most evolved species on the planet. We adapted ourselves and the environment around us over millennia to suit our needs and wants. However, we are yet to accept the differences among ourselves. The dawn of the 21st century has seen us accelerate our efforts towards accepting, recognising and understanding each other, and our differences, in a better way. However, we still have a long way to go. It is my sincere hope that our society becomes truly inclusive.

Mass media has enabled the exposure of various cultures and backgrounds, giving us the opportunity to learn more about each other, our behaviours, preferences, orientations and identities. As this awareness spreads, the willingness to accept each other will hopefully grow. The more people interact with each other across races, religions, cultures and languages, the more they will realise that similarities are greater than differences. Judging people by how they look, behave, or their sexual orientation amounts to disregarding their talents, uniqueness and abilities.

Our uniqueness is our strength. I realised this sometime in 2001. I had moved from India to work at the SAP headquarters in Germany. I was getting to know the people and their culture, and making friends there. My friend circle was slowly growing, and we used to meet frequently for breakfast during the weekends. During one such meeting, I met a lady. Since we happened to sit opposite each other at the breakfast table, I started by introducing myself and talking about India. Like we usually do, I asked her about her hobbies, and she told me that she and her partner were avid trekkers. Without giving it much thought, I made polite enquiries about her partner and asked her if he too was working with her. To which she replied that her partner was not a 'he' but a 'she'. She noticed the surprised look on my face and smiled. I was too embarrassed by my reaction and when I got back home, I reflected deeply on the prejudice and judgement that I was carrying. Back then, India was still conservative and, without my knowledge, I had carried this conservative attitude with me. That was when I decided that I had to remove my subconscious bias and thereafter worked hard to understand people and their sexual orientations. That was the beginning of a long journey of my involvement with the LGBT+ community.

In India, the honourable Supreme Court revoked Section 377 of the Indian Penal Code on 6th September 2018, which marked the beginning of a new era for the LGBT+ community. That judgment signalled that we are taking the right steps towards becoming a more inclusive society. The youth are our beacon of hope for a beautiful future. The LGBT+ community's GenZ members, who will be joining the workforce in a few years, should take pride in their identity, without letting the negativity in the words or actions of others impact their ability to follow their passion with diligence. Corporate India is changing radically, in realising that diversity and inclusion are crucial to success. There is so much work to be done, in various sectors for LGBT+ inclusion, sensitisation and awareness, and that is why it is so essential that GenZ should take charge and move ahead. In this context, it is gratifying that in the Deloitte Global Millennial Survey 2020, the millennials and the GenZ surveyed, before and after the start of COVID-19, said that they have remained focussed on broader societal issues, and are keen to help, drive positive change in their communities and around the world.

At SAP, our commitment to diversity and inclusion is critical to our success. With employees from 150+ nationalities, it is essential that every employee feels free to be their authentic selves for our company to perform its best. We embrace and encourage different perspectives. Our strength lies in the unique combination of culture, race, ethnicity, age, gender, sexual orientation, gender identity or expression, physical or mental ability and work-life situations. Our culture of inclusion and focus on the health and well-being of our employees helps ensure that everyone, regardless of their background, feels included. When we collaborate with others who have different points of view, it creates a more splendid mix of ideas and spurs innovation.

Over the last decade, SAP has taken incremental steps towards creating an all-inclusive work environment, where everyone can feel welcome. In 2010, SAP got a perfect score in the Corporate Equality Index created by the Human Rights Campaign, a group that promotes LGBT+ welfare in the US. In 2017, we started Pride@SAP, an initiative that aims to recognise and celebrate LGBT+ culture.

In 2018, SAP was ushered into the list of Top 10 companies in LGBT+ inclusion by Workplace Pride, a non-profit foundation dedicated to improving the lives of lesbian, gay, bisexual, transgender and intersex (LGBTI) people in workplaces across the world. In May 2019, we partnered with Pride Circle, a diversity and inclusion consultancy, that works towards fostering LGBT+ inclusion at workplaces. We also hosted a Pride Circle Meet Up at SAP Labs, India, Whitefield campus in Bengaluru. This was followed up with a celebration of Pride Month in June, with a Pride march held on SAP's campuses across India, which garnered a lot of support from the employees.

In conclusion, I want to stress that capability is not governed by identity. What each of us can do and who we are, might be related at some deeper, intrinsic level. However, as we have been taught since childhood, there is no shortcut to hard work and no compromise for sincerity.

Sreekanth Arimanithaya
Global Talent and Enablement Services Leader,
EY Global Delivery Services

BEING AN ALLY—PRIDE IN BELONGING

A true sense of belonging has a powerful and positive impact on one's professional life, as much as personal. The book 'Ikigai' identifies it as a major contributor to both happiness and longevity. What does a sense of belonging translate to within the workspace? According to me, it is any courageous action we take that goes beyond just words. It is the inclusion of diversity in all forms beyond the numbers. It is a cultural fabric which goes beyond the policy framework.

My beliefs as an ally and an individual have deeply influenced my experiences. I have often spoken about my journey from being a chronically shy youngster in Kerala to leading business/functions in large organisations. My journey is scattered with struggles to overcome unconscious biases, not just of society at large, but my own. The first step is to understand yourself and find your own purpose. Always feel free to push yourself to be the best version of yourself, in the manner you desire to be. I have however invested in my ability to communicate and tell stories by overcoming stage fright.

The second factor is, if I can be my authentic self at work—whatever it may be, and the organisation is receptive to what

I bring to the table, that is an incredible feeling. A feeling of belonging.

This is the understanding I try to bring into my role as a sponsor. It is also true that, as a larger society, we have seen a heartening stride being taken in creating both awareness and safe spaces for the LGBT+ community. But we still have a long way to go, and every step in the direction is a giant leap in shaping the workplace narrative.

The biggest mind block that we need to overcome as leaders is to approach this with numbers and statistics. The idea is not to make an inexhaustive list of diversities, but to build a culture that can accommodate all and obliterate the need to have a list. Inclusion is not complete unless you look at the whole spectrum of legal, social and cultural aspects. This enables you to build an environment where every individual can bring their authentic self to work, irrespective of their educational background, financial status, gender, sexual identity, cognitive abilities, language, race, religion and ethnicity.

So, the simplest solution to me, that merges both my roles as a leader and an individual, was to become an LGBT+ ally. My journey as an ally has been eye-opening and has given me a great sense of satisfaction. Initially, I started off by making myself more aware of what it means to take on this role. I started noticing my biases and consciously reached out to people to understand what support means to them. Through my journey, I learnt coming out is not only about the family and society, but more about accepting one's identity, which is a big step. This experience has made me think of my privileges and how I want to ensure every person lives comfortably, irrespective of their gender and sexual identity. To me, being an ally does not mean someone who is completely aware and knows everything about the LGBT+ community. It just means someone who is ready to help, understand and stand up for people from the community.

This sense of community needs to grow, until we all become a conscious and mindful group that is collectively working towards an inclusive society. Organisations can play a key role in enabling this. By creating ally networks within the system, we can make inclusion a natural part of the workplace. In addition to inclusive policies, organisations should also show zero tolerance towards discrimination. As a leader and ally, I am determined to strengthen the strong emphasis EY puts on inclusion, and to continue to make GDS (Global Delivery Services) a safe space which encourages people to bring their authentic selves to work.

Yes, a lot of us are ready and willing to take on the baton of being an ally. This is a great sign, but we must ensure this also reflects in our day-to-day behaviour—breaking myths, shattering biases, shunning stereotypes and really standing up to help when we are required to. I am ready to take this responsibility to build momentum, to consistently and collectively push for inclusion by being vocal, relentless and visible, both in the workspace, and in my community.

You can make a difference too, just take the first step.

The views reflected in this article are the views of the author and do not necessarily reflect the views of the global EY organisation or its member firms.

Sudhir Shenoy
CEO and Country President,
Dow Chemical International Pvt. Ltd.

I grew up in Mumbai (then: Bombay), a city that can be called the melting pot of cultures since time immemorial. When I was very young, my parents moved from Mangalore to Mumbai, where my father set up his transport business.

Since childhood, I have been observing the importance of family values around me. "Together-stronger" was the motto with which we all strode ahead, facing all that came on our way with a smile. Coming from a humble background, my childhood was normal.

There was no one particular moment which opened my eyes (and mind) to inclusion and diversity. Growing up in a multi-cultural city, you already have exposure to people from all walks of life. So one would think that you become accepting of ideologies, beliefs and backgrounds that are much different to what you were brought up with, but this is not necessarily true always. While we had a reasonable gender diversity in the school classroom, we had no one with a visible disability, and, of course, gender fluidity was not even a part of our lexicon then. We did have the regular presence of transgender people in the streets and in local trains, but it was not something that was talked about openly and or in a constructive fashion, as I realised much later.

As I grew in my career with Dow, I started participating in various employee resource groups (ERGs) at my workplace. Gradually, I was getting more inquisitive. I wanted to read more and needed to understand many other aspects of diversity and inclusion. So I educated myself on disability, gender parity and the LGBT+ community. I started with exploring it on my own on the internet, then I moved on to books and movies. Furthermore, I attended forums and participated in seminars and conferences where people from the LGBT+ community spoke about their experiences. Some of these encounters blossomed into friendships and that is when I got a closer glimpse of the struggles faced by the people and had a stunning realisation of our desensitisation, and the inhuman treatment meted out to this community.

For starters, we have normalised using some of the words used for the LGBT+ community members, as swear words in our day-to-day life. Weirdly, that is something we have all grown up hearing and using and no one ever corrected anybody about it. It might not be a conscious retort, simply because it is so deeply ingrained in our psyche as 'normal'. But it is not normal. It demonstrates our bias against the people of the community. To make matters worse, I realised the overpowering impact it had on me as well. For all the great inclusiveness I believed in, and was championing, I had also been brainwashed into it. This had to change!

As if these moments of gradual awakening were not enough, life sent across a huge eye-opener for me one day. I was driving down to my cousin's house for a family function when I stopped at a traffic signal. Suddenly, a transgender person came knocking on my car window, seeking alms. By this time, I was completely conscious about my behaviour and knew they should not be treated differently. Our normal conditioning is to shoo them away quickly. At times, we even roll our windows up to show our disinterest. But this time, I wanted to be different. So, I rolled down the window with a smile and tried talking to them, "Hey, what is your name?"

While I know people usually do not indulge in conversations with them, leave alone asking about their name or well-being, I wanted to do so. I wanted to treat them with dignity and respect. Unbeknownst to me, my attempts to make a difference were falling flat. The person was not interested in any conversation. It was very evident in their tone, as they clapped harder to get my attention back to business and asked for money. That was it!

She left as soon as I handed her some money. However, I was stupefied. A million questions crossed my mind at that moment—"Was I wrong in my behaviour? All I wanted to show the person, was that I cared. Someone cared for them. Maybe my method to show my concern wasn't right?"

And that is when it struck me, they are not used to politeness. What have we done? Over the years, we have dehumanised this community so badly, that they no longer consider themselves a part of society. It would not be wrong to say that this interaction accelerated my journey towards becoming an ally.

Back home, we have been having conversations about this for quite a while. Still, I cannot say I have managed to convert all my family members into allies. Some of my relatives and extended family members are still uncomfortable with homosexuality. They think that homosexuality is a matter of choice. On the other hand, my children are absolutely comfortable with it all. Perhaps, I can give some of the credit to their international education here. Even in secondary classes, they are surrounded with friends and classmates who are already 'out' to their family.

Sometimes I feel that they are far more advanced than me when it comes to inclusion and diversity. The ease with which they talk about their classmates being gay or lesbian is comforting.

In a way, at work and at home, I am consciously trying to bring in a change. Though I have not yet succeeded in doing so completely, the small steps I take every day matter the most. Like that one time, when I had visited a restaurant in Vashi where the entire staff comprised of transgender persons. It was rejuvenating to see that and it encouraged me to meet the owner, to discuss and understand the workings closely. In the long run, I want to have some of the LGBT+ community members as employees or contractors at our offices.

Educated people like us have an added responsibility of sensitising people around us. We cannot afford to be passive allies now. Silence is no longer an option. We need to be vocal about the LGBT+ community as much as we can. And this is not just about attending forums, conferences or seminars. It is also about interacting with them at parties, board meetings, social get-togethers, family functions, etc.

In every role I play—that of a father, brother, son, husband, manager—I try to carry these values and also spread them around to everyone I am closely working with. I agree that it has not been easy. Undoing years of social conditioning is going to take time, but we need to keep making efforts. That is how we will be able to bring the change we want to see.

We need to break the taboo surrounding the LGBT+ community and encourage discussions concerning their issues. There will be questions, there will be doubts—but we have to be patient with those people and take them through this process of awakening. We have been there ourselves, so we are the best people to help others undergo this process of awakening. Some might take more time to do so, while some might understand it all in a jiffy. The key is to be patient and persistent, without being hesitant.

At times, when I feel down, I always remember my childhood motto of "Together stronger". This is exactly what will take us forward, as a community even now. When we co-exist respectfully, taking into consideration our differences that is when we will grow as individuals, as a society and as a country.

Sudish Panicker

Managing Director and Head,
BNY Mellon International Operations,
India

I am a proud South Indian by birth with deep East Indian values through formative years and a profound West Indian influence on my professional life. I grew up in a fairly affluent neighbourhood in Kolkata, where playing and hanging out together in street corners was part of our cultural heritage. It was perhaps during my first year of chartered accountancy when during one of our regular gatherings, a boy from our group hesitantly opened up about his sexual orientation. Everyone was rather naive, as I distinctly remember, so at that moment, none of us knew how to react. We were in complete shock, unable to accept this significant detail about his life. However, our naivety caused us to exclude him and cut off all contact with him- we literally avoided him in the group.

Many years later, when I moved to Hyderabad for work, I unexpectedly ran into him and realised that we were now co-workers! For me, this reunion was especially exciting; to think that two childhood friends who grew up together were now united to work together in a different city! It was only when we started talking that I remembered how we had parted. In fact, he vividly recalled how he was shunned by not only our group, but also many other friends and associates, family members and even by his sister whom he used to consider his best friend!

He then spoke about a person whom he had met, who became his confidant, mentor, advisor and 'ally'. He later introduced me to the person, and that meeting had a lasting impression on me regarding the power of being an ally. A big shout-out and deep respect for this individual for taking a stand against all odds, going the extra mile for his friend, even initiating conversations with his family and friends in the neighbourhood, fighting for his rights to be heard and included. This is when the impact of 'allyship' dawned on me.

This, however, became much more real when I first learnt about the BNY Mellon 'PRISM Ally Programme', that engages people to actively support LGBT+ employees and communities.

The above experience has helped me understand that an ally can be anyone who supports, empowers, or advocates against the oppression of a group or its members. Being a good 'ally', starts with stepping back and listening to the people you want to help; to amplify their voice and commit to long-term 'allyship'. It also entails aiming for a long-lasting, tangible change within communities.

At BNY Mellon, we believe that there is no greater value than the freedom to be yourself. We do not want our people to cope, we want them to grow in a diverse, inclusive environment, where they can achieve their full potential. Supported by a strong network of allies, PRISM, BNY Mellon's LGBT+ Employee Resource Group (ERG), promotes an open and supportive environment for all lesbian, gay, bisexual, transgender, queer or questioning (LGBTQ+) individuals. The programme has made a good start in creating awareness, encouraging our employees to be active allies and partners within the company, industry and in their own communities. Since we began our journey in 2017, over 5,000 employees in India including the leadership, have been proactively participating in various events organised for Pride. While a lot of the ground work has been done, the proof of the pudding is in its eating. Here we mean changing people's minds and hearts. Many of our teams are now comfortable hiring people from the LGBT+ community and creating an inclusive workplace where they can thrive, shine, feel valued, respected and empowered.

Today, I feel there is more acknowledgement and acceptance within parts of our educated society. However, this topic still remains a taboo outside certain sections of the population. Unfortunately, this covers a large part of India. That is where the real challenge remains. How do we bridge the gap between these two worlds? As responsible citizens, there is so much more that we can do to create a comfortable environment where we can support, motivate and encourage the LGBT+ community. We need to take the conversation ahead and beyond, apart from just creating awareness and dialogues.

I encourage each of you to reach out to one another, lend an ear and provide a shoulder without judgement and bias. The world around us will only be richer with diversity. However, that diversity can flourish only with inclusion.

Now is the time to care selflessly about each other, stay focussed and stay connected. Let us show our collective strength by continuing to be allies and advocates for each other.

Dr Sukanyya Misra
Senior Vice President
India Technology Hub, Mastercard

Rabindranath Tagore's poem *"Where the mind is without fear..."* has resonated with me and has been one of my guiding lights.

I grew up in Calcutta (Kolkata now) in an environment seeped with art, theatre and culture, typically how most Bengalis grow up. Coming from a family of doctors and academicians, education was a priority in our house and so there were certain unsaid rules that revolved around knowledge building and learning. My family always taught us that education helps in the growth of the mind, opens up rigid belief systems and helps get rid of prejudices.

This childhood learning helped me adapt during college days, far away from home in the State University of New York (SUNY) Buffalo in the US. Living with a diverse group of people from varied backgrounds was an enriching experience, making me realise how beautiful different cultures are and how limited my exposure towards the world outside had been.

Our college campus was a vibrant space, also where I had my first exposure to the LGBT+ movement and subsequent interaction with the growing community that organized many activities. Being on the same campus, I understood how our differences made us whole as a society. Diversity makes this world so much more interesting, and without it, human existence is boring and mundane.

Today, society and corporates understand the importance of diversity and inclusion as it brings in varied perspectives and outlooks necessary to innovate and evolve. It is a belief that our differences enable us to be a better team, leading to better decisions, driving innovation and delivering business results. While things have greatly evolved in recent years, there is still a need to create more awareness. Behind this term, LGBT+, there are people—our friends, family, colleagues, etc., and there is a need to build a safe and inclusive space for all.

At an individual level, it is critical to inculcate the mindset of inclusion that is built on the belief that diversity is important for the progress of any society. As a leader, I strive to build understanding of the current and traditional barriers to diverse representation of people at all levels and continue to put into motion programmes and support systems to overcome those barriers.

At a corporate level, we at Mastercard aim to create meaningful connections, inspire acceptance and cultivate a culture where we all belong. For us, inclusion means achieving a work-life environment where all individuals are treated fairly and respectfully, have equal access to opportunities, and resources, and can contribute fully to the organization and the larger society. As an enabler of commerce across 210 countries and 50 million merchants, Mastercard's products and services cater to all segments of the world's population. Our culture of diversity sparks innovation and inclusion encourages collaboration—this is key to the multitude of payment solutions and our expanding business.

Our PRIDE business resource groups (BRGs) work towards

Dr Sukanyya Misra

driving awareness, sensitizing our people towards the LGBT+ community and their issues, and promoting acceptance. We recently launched an informative training programme for our employees to build mindfulness around LGBT+ individuals. In this programme, we discuss their lifestyle and the challenges faced by them, encourage allyship, demystify any stereotypes and emphasize our company's gender inclusive people policies.

We have put in concerted efforts to create a safe and supportive environment, which embraces diversity and promotes an employee's ability to contribute to the business objectives regardless of their sexual orientation, gender identity or expression. We believe an inclusive workplace is one where people feel encouraged to bring their 'whole selves' to work. Between voicing diverse points of view and finding a sense of connection with others, this is what makes inclusion real.

At a community level, we are championing a future of unconditional acceptance because we feel that is priceless. We work closely with NGO partners to support LGBT+ communities and provide them with resources and equal opportunities. For many in the LGBT+ community, the name on their credit, debit or prepaid card does not reflect their true identity. As a result, for the transgender and non-binary community, the card in their pocket misrepresents their true identity when they are shopping and going about their daily life. To address this challenge, we introduced the True Name™ feature that allows chosen names to appear on the cards, helping ease a major sensitive issue for the community.

Celebrating acceptance is inherent in our company's DNA, and we believe we have an important role to play in championing acceptance for all. To show our support, we built an Acceptance Street, New York, through which we hope to recognise the entirety of the LGBT+ community and emphasize the importance of supporting inclusiveness for all.

We understand and appreciate all things that make us different, and similar, are assets. None of us are a carbon copy of the other. Therefore, we are all diverse.

When you surround yourself with people who do not look like you, do not walk like you, do not talk like you, do not have the same experiences as you, that is when new ideas are sparked, and innovation happens.

Decency has long been central to who we are as a company and everything we do at Mastercard. We have worked for many years to promote inclusion and equality, but we still have more to do to confront and combat any kind of discrimination and racism in all its forms.

Suneeta Rao
Indipop Singer, Dancer, Actress

"Your life is a sham till you can shout out, I am what I am!" The strains of that proud and joyous melody wafted through the doors of a tiny apartment in Cuffe Parade as I ascended the stairs with a mix of trepidation and heady excitement. This was a new world for me. I was at the brink of stardom at 15; I had just landed my first lead role as Sandy in the Indian adaptation of the iconic teen musical, 'GREASE'. The world of theatre was about to inundate my life with stage, song, dance, lights, mischief and the warm smell of theatre green rooms. I was on first name basis with my colleagues who were all double my age, and I was exposed to much more than a girl with my middle class 'Matunga background' could have dreamt of.

The door burst open and I was struck by the energy and joie de vivre of the person in front of me. I was swooped up in a rush of welcoming hugs and kisses, and instantly found myself, to my pleasant bewilderment, dancing with a bunch of strangers... all men...all gay...all happy and high on sheer passion. There was no substance abuse, no judgment and no questions asked. The walls of the room were adorned with the vibrant posters of Moulin Rouge, La Cage aux Folles and RuPaul. For the first time in my life, I felt I was a grown up...and free.

This was my first exposure to the gay community. The

man whose house I was in, died a few years later of a disease I had no idea about at the time. In the years to follow I met and got close to some of the most witty, generous, hilarious and loving gay people I have ever known. From dancers and choreographers, to make-up men and fashion designers, many of them were actually like brothers to me and continue to be, to this day. Although I hesitate to use the term 'brother', because our relationship never had anything to do with their sexuality or mine. We were just human beings, attracted to each other purely for giving and receiving love and friendship. My not being gay never affected that.

But what broke my heart was those who had not "come out"—not even to me, even though I was so close to them. We both knew the truth but out of compassion and sensitivity I did not pry and just accepted them as they were. I think that was why they were so comfortable with me. I would find them hanging out with other gay people at the shoot or backstage. I would feel comfortable changing clothes in the same room as them while laughing hysterically over some silly joke, all along not even giving their sexual orientation a thought. But soon I started to hear horror stories of queer bashing and my skin would crawl. I lost respect for friends and colleagues who spoke in judgment of the community.

I was never taught any of this—it was all instinctual. Why on earth should I consider myself in any way superior to anyone just because they are different from me? There were also those who came out only to me and no one else. I never gave this a second thought all these years.

It was only when I was approached to pen down my thoughts that I started to think about this. Why me?

A lot of it may have had to do with my persona as a pop

Suneeta Rao

star in the 1990s and the release of the now iconic video of my song 'Paree Hoon Main'. Perhaps it was because I was a young woman with a strong image and a mind of my own, in a country like ours, with all its patriarchy and religious dogmas, who embarked fearlessly and with no apologies on an independent career in Indipop. Without succumbing to the lure of Bollywood, I made bold choices with regard to the content of my music and videos—be it domestic abuse (*Dehka Dehka*), anti-smoking (*Dhuan*), anti-greed (*Paisa*) or anti-sex selection (*Sun Zara*). In doing so, I believe something about me seemed to give the community a sense of pride and motivated them to fearlessly be themselves and find joy in it. So many homosexual men and women have approached me and talked about how my music (especially songs like *Kesaria*, *Ab Ke Baras* and of course *Paree Hoon Main*) has liberated them and become almost a sort of anthem for them. Some are close friends now, making what we have a seamless, human equation and a growing universe of solidarity.

This has moved me immensely and I am honoured to have been called an 'ally' and to be given the opportunity to share my experiences and thoughts in this very important book.

Having said that, I do not think we are at war. But I would like to believe there are no enemies. I always thought that the sign of the devil was 666. But the real evil was 377.

Surekha Shenoy
Corporate Leader

When we meet people, our mind immediately 'slots' them into categories and our behaviour is guided by this categorisation. This is social stereotyping and it typically stems out of our unconscious biases. All of us would have been victims of such behaviour in some form at different points in our lives. My own experiences have made me acutely aware of the need to avoid such a bias.

In my own early years, in a different context, I realised how difficult it was to pretend and play a role versus being one's authentic self. Having someone to speak to and to receive support from would have made a world of difference to me and my potential. I chose to be an ally to the LGBT+ community to demonstrate that diversity and inclusion will make it a better world for all of us. For me, being an ally is about being visible and vocal in supporting the under-represented or marginalised communities apart from being actively involved in inclusion initiatives.

It starts with making the effort to understand the community and the nuances. It also includes not shying from asking questions appropriately and familiarising oneself with acceptable norms of behaviour. One may end up making mistakes in the beginning. Graciously apologise when that happens and continue to make an effort to educate yourself with LGBT+ issues and lingo.

Drop your preconceived notions, and try to build a trusting relationship with members of the community to know their perspectives and challenges.

When speaking to someone from the community, accept their perspective and listen, without making assumptions. Be compassionate. Be sensitive when they reach out—whether it is just to chat or for any suggestions they make to create a more inclusive environment, it is possible you could make it happen.

I believe actions speak louder than words. Show support by using an ally card at your desk, wear a purple ribbon, participate in important milestones like the International Day Against Homophobia, Biphobia, Interphobia and Transphobia (IDAHOBIT) and Pride Month. Thus, participate in events that celebrate the community. Be a confidante for those who want to 'come out'. Do not out anyone without their explicit permission. It is also important to challenge stereotypes and inappropriate jokes and comments about the community.

Garner more support and spread the word like you would do for all good thoughts and ideas. I believe a good ally also encourages people to become allies and expands the sphere of influence.

Bring up the next generation to be LGBT+ inclusive. For me that meant having conversations with my 13-year-old daughter, who has since then made the effort to understand the community. I was proud when she displayed the Pride flag as her screensaver during the Pride Month this year.

Most of my friends and family understand that I am an ally because I never miss an opportunity to express my views in a positive, meaningful way in relevant conversations.

Awareness, training, policies and broader education can create a meaningful change in any culture, whether it is in a corporate environment or an institution garnering support and directing efforts on sensitisation. Allies have a key role to play in creating an open and non-judgmental environment. They are someone with whom LGBT+ colleagues can build trusting relationships. I have tried to share experiences and best practices across companies, institutions and broader society in general.

I have personally grown as an individual, as I have made many friends who are from the community. The relationship and bond that I share with them is just as unique as they are. When there is collaboration and engagement at all levels of society, we will begin to see real change.

Ever since I became a vocal public ally through forums and initiatives, I found members of the community opening up to me. I have gained friends simply by being there when they shared their joys, aspirations and challenges. Quite a few of them have chosen to come out to me even before their family and friends. To my very pleasant surprise, this went beyond the confines of the corporate environment where I had focussed a lot of energy. I am glad I have been able to create that confidence and trust to allow open dialogue, and be there for those who need me. It has helped me grow as an individual and be respectful of perspectives and diversities beyond sexuality.

As today's college students prepare to join the workplace, I would appeal to them to remain open-minded. They should share their ideas to shape their workplace into a place where everyone feels a strong sense of belonging and can make a contribution. I recommend that they actively look for companies with an inclusive culture, where managers seek out diverse perspectives and ideas to drive business success. Be a role model. Support colleagues from under-represented or marginalised groups, so as to build a society together, where everyone can be their authentic selves without any judgment or prejudice.

Most companies have active employee relations groups focussed on diversity and inclusion. Look to engage with such initiatives and contribute actively to drive positive change. If there is not one, look to create a group with like-minded individuals and get support from the organisation.

If the company you join supports public advocacy, look to actively volunteer and help.

As cliché as it may sound, "Be the change you want to see".

Tanisha Vinod
Student, LGBT+ Ally,
Chocolate aficionado

A few years ago, on our way to church on a Sunday, we stopped at a traffic signal. I saw someone who looked like a man, but was dressed in a sari, asking my mother for some money. At that time, I did not know anything about the transgender community, so I asked my mom who they were and she explained to me about transgenders, the challenges they faced and how they were ostracised by society. I was speechless. After a moment of silence and processing what my mother had just told me, I asked her, "Oh, but it's okay to be one, ma? Right?"

My mother has had a significant influence on me and I am blessed to have her in my life. She was the first one to tell me about the LGBT+ community, and being the head of diversity and inclusion (D&I) initiatives at her workplace, she has been an ally for a long time. She told me about the Genderbread Person, an online resource for information about the LGBT+ community, and the difference between gender expression, identity, biological sex and sexual orientation. She also told me if I see someone who is from the community or someone who looks different from others, I should not make fun of them. Over the years, I have seen movies where there are insensitive gay jokes and I just wonder why we cannot be accepting of all.

I have been following many celebrities and YouTubers who are LGBT+ and I admire how they have achieved so much in spite of the disdain they face regularly. James Charles, the popular make-up artist is one of them. Talk show host Ellen DeGeneres is another person I deeply admire.

At home, we often talk about LGBT+ rights and my mom often tells us about the events that she had attended that support and promote equal opportunities for the community.

At school, some people just make fun of LGBT+ people. If friends of the same-sex hold hands, or even if they hug, they are mocked for it. I find that to be very inappropriate and insensitive. If we are going to mock our friends like that, how would anyone come out and survive in such a hostile environment?

As cis-teens, we go through many body acceptance issues. Am I too fat, thin, short or tall? I imagine it could be worse for LGBT+ teens. They would have many questions about "who they are" and would struggle to navigate those doubts. I strongly believe that we need to treat everyone with respect. Some people are simply homophobic because they have been mostly ignorant and we need to educate them. We need to start talking about the LGBT+ community openly in schools and colleges, telling people that it is natural. We need to treat everyone equally. We should screen movies, participate in Pride marches and have people who are LGBT+ share their stories with us. Then, this world will be a better place for all of us!

To everyone who is LGBT+, especially teens, I would like to say "be the person you want to be". Love yourself more than anyone else and do not try to fit in like everybody. You were born to stand out! Be brave and strong. Do not let anyone judge you. Go live your dreams. LGBT+ is who you are, so

equALLY

shine your light on everyone. Love every inch of yourself and do not change for anyone.

Tanvi Choksi
Head–Human Resources, India and
JLL Business Services, Global, JLL

The brand promise "Achieve Ambitions" of JLL is lived with its people. Employees are the firm's biggest strength, and their ambitions, both professional and personal, are encouraged and nurtured until accomplishment. JLL provides equal opportunities to all irrespective of gender, geography or generation. Diversity and inclusion is promoted within the firm at all levels. With over 11,000 employees, what accelerates our growth is the power of One JLL. Together, we celebrate our unique backgrounds, thoughts, perspectives, skills and experiences.

Personally, I am passionate about enabling our people to achieve their professional and personal ambitions. Thanks to my team and the business leaders, together, we have structured multiple programmes that enable our people's growth and comfort within the firm. Not just this, we have also tied up with the government to create unique programmes for skill development. Our initiatives focus on the 3Gs— Gender, Geography and Generation to ensure inclusiveness at the workplace. Gradual return to work policy, flexi hours, mentorship for women leaders, allies/support groups, in-office babyterias and creche facilities, are few of the offerings for our people across genders and levels.

Our hearts and spaces are always open for the LGBT+ community, and hence, we have multiple employment avenues for them as well. Understanding the complexities and the sentiments of the LGBT+ community, we conducted a pilot run to hire LGBT+ people in our Mumbai office in 2018 (even before Section 377 of the Indian Penal Code was scrapped by the Supreme Court). The selection process was purely merit-based, and we received multiple applications from the community. The selected candidate was finally absorbed in the HR team in Mumbai and later posted to Hyderabad (her hometown) on her request.

As part of our diversity and inclusion (D&I) initiatives, special sessions are held for our people across levels and geographies to sensitise them about components of sexual orientation and gender identity. Every year we celebrate D&I Week, also called 'Celebrating Who We Are'. As part of these celebrations, a day is dedicated to celebrating the beautiful rainbow colours. I remember, during the D&I Week celebrations last year, one of our LGBT+ employees opened up and spoke about how before joining us, she was facing problems in getting a job due to social stigma and discrimination against transgender people. She feared not being accepted in the team and her gender coming in the way of her work being appreciated. However, the day she joined us, that day became the start of her progressive journey, personally as well as professionally.

We go beyond the LGBT+ culture too. Specially abled people are close to us, as they possess unique ability to create magic with their thoughts and skills. With many specially abled employees on board, we ensure that the rest of the employees know how to interact with them correctly. For that, we conduct sensitisation workshops regularly. All this displays how inclusive and diverse we are as a firm. However, to keep this culture alive, it is essential to have people who promote the culture of inclusion. We call them Workplace Allies. Such bunch of our people align themselves with other colleagues to make sure they are heard and included. For the LGBT+ people, they play a significant role in helping them realise their potential.

The LGBT+ people face many hurdles in accessing the healthcare that they need. In keeping with our vision of providing equal opportunity for all, the firm offers gender-neutral benefits like medical coverage for all employees, including same-sex partners. We have addressed the restroom issue for LGBT+ employees at work by providing gender-neutral restrooms with gender-neutral bathroom sign options.

For me, D&I means to be understood, embraced and respected. Here is my favourite story that keeps motivating me to make a difference in the world.

Once upon a time, an old man used to go by the ocean to do his writing. He had the habit of walking on the beach before he begun his work. One day, as he was walking along the shore, he looked down the beach and saw a human figure dancing. He smiled to himself at the thought of someone who would dance in the day, and so, he walked faster to catch up.

As he got closer, he noticed that the figure was that of a young man who was not dancing at all. The young man was reaching down to the shore, picking up small objects and throwing them into the ocean. The man came closer still and called out, "Good morning! May I ask what is it that you are doing?" The young man paused, looked up, and replied, "Throwing starfish into the ocean." "I must ask, then, why are you throwing starfish into the ocean?" asked the somewhat startled the old man. To this, the young man replied, "The sun is up, and the tide is going out. If I don't throw them in, they'll die."

Upon hearing this, the old man commented, "But, young man, do you not realise that there are miles and miles of this beach and there are starfish all along every mile? You can't possibly make a difference!" At this, the young man bent down, picked up yet another starfish, and threw it into the ocean. As it met the water, he said, "It made a difference for that one."

I truly believe that while we may not be able to change the world, we can make a difference to one person at a time. On some days, trying to make a difference is hard. It can feel like our small efforts to change our little corner of the world might get lost in a sea of challenges. Being a change-maker is hard. It is never-ending, and the waves of oppression can be relentless. However, always remember: You can make a difference!

I support equal rights. I support Pride!

Taru Dahiya
Director, Asia Pacific,
Google Cloud, Google

I can never compare my own gender-biased experiences with those of the members of the LGBT+ community, who may have experienced discrimination, in some form in their daily lives. However, I have always been an advocate of inclusion and equal rights—be it in my own extended family, where benevolent sexism commonly prevailed while I was growing up, or in the schools that I attended.

My journey towards allyship started with no intentional effort and was entirely accidental, but what I do today as an ally is deliberate and aimed at making a difference. During a work trip to an Asian country, a few years ago, I met an employee whom I had previously interviewed for Google.

During our conversation, I congratulated the team member on the positive impact of their work on our business. Suddenly, this team member began to cry. As I paused to comprehend what was happening, the person hugged and thanked me for hiring them into Google, and how I made them feel like they were an important part of the team. I learned that this person was treated very differently in their previous company for being gay. The mental stress and discrimination forced them to leave that job. While I struggled to find the right words to say to the person, as a Googler for the past 15 years, I wanted them to know that Google is an inclusive workplace where employees could be themselves. I offered them my support and a window to reach out to me anytime, if they wanted to talk again.

For months, this incident lingered on my mind, and I reflected deeply on how privileged I was. I recognised how important it was, not just for myself, but for everyone to be accepted for who they are. I had a burning question: "What is the use of this privilege, if I don't use it to support and alleviate the problems of the marginalised?" I have been active in various employee resource groups (ERGs) at Google, helping women uplift themselves and feel empowered; however, I kept wondering, "What if I could do the same for the LGBT+ community?"

This thought led me to join the Pride group at Google India ERG and I started attending various panel discussions, events and workshops. These initiatives were eye-opening for me, as I got to listen to the personal stories and challenges faced by individuals from the community. I acknowledged that I have so much to learn and gradually built empathy towards their life's experiences to become a stronger and an active ally.

Today, my commitment to LGBT+ inclusion is an important part of my personal and professional journey. It goes beyond workplace policies. With the strong focus on diversity, equity and inclusion that Google puts into the work culture, one can truly make a difference in how the LGBT+ community experience their workplace. In my opinion, it does not take a lot to bring about meaningful change. Knowing this, I am hopeful about expanding our allies' network and further strengthening the journey of inclusion. I have now stepped up to become an executive sponsor for Pride at Google India ERG and, trust me, it is one of the most satisfying roles I play at Google. There is no

Taru Dahiya

well-paved road for the LGBT+ community in India, but let me assure you that we are making progress. If the word 'world' is too big for you, then start small—try to contribute towards creating an inclusive workplace and an accepting neighbourhood! Be an active ally!

Tina Muthanna
Vice President–Business Analytics and Research, Fidelity India

WHEN PRIDE IS MORE THAN JUST RAINBOWS

The month of June went by in a blur of colours! It was after all Pride Month. Across the globe, there was much celebration by the LGBT+ community and their allies. Closer home, in the workplace it was heartening to see the engagement and participation in various activities organised by our Pride Employee Resource Group (ERG).

Looking back, I am proud of my journey in allying with Pride. It began at a workshop in the office that sensitised us to unconscious biases and how predisposed we were to judge people without understanding. It made me introspect on how aware I had been, how curious I was to know more and how far I would go to stand up for something that could be categorised as a basic right of any individual.

The more aware I became, the deeper the realisation dawned upon me about how unfair things were. Just imagine what it must be like to be closeted, to bear the burden of concealing one's identity due to the fear of loss—the loss of friendships and career opportunities.

As the executive sponsor of the Pride ERG at Fidelity India, I am often asked if there are guidelines for being a better ally.

Tina Muthanna

Here is what I have learned:

1. Walk the talk. Call out the hecklers, nip coloured jokes and remarks in the bud, and show your support for the cause through your actions and words.
2. Accept that we all need space and privacy. Just like you would never probe a straight person for intimate details, 'curiosity' is no excuse for asking an LGBT+ community member about details of things that do not concern us.
3. If you are participating in a Pride event, try to understand its origin. It is more than just a parade or a party. And you are a guest at the party. How you behave after the music has stopped blaring and the glitter has washed off the sidewalks is as important as how much you enjoy yourself during the event.

We have come a long way since the Stonewall Riots when the gay community in the US asserted themselves against police injustice 50 years ago. We have seen much progress in the cause of inclusion today. However, we have a long way to go. There are still places in this country, and around the world, where coming out faces the risk of being kept out. The least we can do is foster an environment that allows for everyone to bring their whole selves to work and feel free, safe and supported.

There is already a certain vulnerability around revealing your authentic self. Why make it harder?

So, celebrate who you are and let it inspire Pride!

Trinetri Arora
Corporate leader

Generation Z is in a unique position where LGBT+ has been brought out of the proverbial closet and has been made mainstream in India. Corporates across the board are coming out as visible allies in support of the community. The emphasis is on an individual bringing their whole selves to the workplace and, therefore, being able to contribute and develop their innate talents appropriately.

My advice is to be yourself unequivocally and have an open mindset. Take the time to participate in the inclusive culture that has been built and defined in corporate India today. An example of an inclusive workplace would be one where policies, infrastructure and culture are developed to respect an individual for their contribution without the influence of any bias. This includes executing firmwide training sessions aimed at sensitising and reinforcing a culture of absolute inclusion. This ensures fair treatment of employees, irrespective of their gender or sexual orientation.

The Indian corporate landscape has evolved to recognise and reward individuals based on their talents, efforts and skill sets. However, we require the current generation to hold us accountable to improve our standards of inclusion. In the coming years, the contributions made by the current generation will redefine inclusion both in the workplace and in society as a whole.

Vedica Saxena

Project Director,
Tagore International School

I reside in Delhi where I work as a project director with Tagore International School. My job has allowed me the opportunity to conduct gender sensitisation workshops with young adults. I have also been a panellist and speaker on important social issues. I had been a model for a decade in the past. I have also been a freelance soft skills trainer with schools, colleges and corporates, and a master of ceremonies (emcee). In 2017, I decided to pursue my passion for writing and started blogging. I have written more than 100 articles for platforms like Momspresso, Women's Web, Fuzia, Blogchatter and BlogAdda, among others. I am also a TEDx speaker.

I always believe that the number of lives that you impact are the only deeds that eventually matter. I am a straightforward person who believes in voicing her opinion no matter what. I believe in standing up for the rights of others. I was blessed to be raised in a family that encouraged open dialogues, so there was ample room for healthy conversations and decision making. Despite this, I was not exposed to the LGBT+ community until I was 18 years old.

I studied in a convent school for girls where we were taught by nuns. We never even had any male students to interact with, so forget about discussions or awareness around gender and sex. We only received basic information in our school's biology books about male and female sexual organs.

I was first exposed to the LGBT+ community when I started modelling at the age of 18. I had some models and designer friends from the industry and that is when I learnt about sexuality. However, that was not an in-depth learning. It was based on what I could gauge or understand from my perspective of all that I was seeing about a person on the outside. And of course, in those days the exposure in school or college was not like it is today. Even parents can participate in these talks at some homes and schools right now, it was unthinkable then.

However, many are not open and comfortable about these conversations. I really wish this changes soon. Luckily, my parents were always welcoming of transgender people and treated them as equals whenever we encountered them on streets. This is how I learned to respect them.

My story of becoming an ally started when I joined Tagore International School, Vasant Vihar, more than one-and-a-half years ago as a project director. As part of my role, I head multiple social awareness campaigns which are student-driven. One such campaign is Breaking Barriers. It is a sustainable human rights awareness initiative which started in 2013, with the aim of sensitising the youth, especially school students, about LGBT+ rights. Under my leadership and training, the members conduct gender sensitisation sessions in schools and colleges across the city to spread awareness about sexuality and gender equality, bullying and discrimination at school level as part of the campaign.

Soon after, I had started collaborating with like-minded people like Prince Manvendra Singh Gohil—the chairman of Lakshya Trust, Parmesh Shahani—founder of the Godrej

India Culture Lab, Harish Iyer—co-founder of the Jimme Foundation and mental health practitioner, Richa Vashista. I have also had the opportunity to work with organisations like the Canadian High Commission, the Naz Foundation, Keshav Suri Foundation and Lakshya Trust as part of the campaign. So far, we have sensitised more than 4,000 students and 35 schools. Today, many of these institutions seek our help to initiate similar campaigns in their institutes.

Being an ally has definitely broadened my perspective and enriched my thought process. I was touched when I started interacting with people from the community and learnt about some of their hardships. I wanted to create a positive change in two ways. First, by changing their situation, making them financially and morally independent and second, by spreading awareness about the reality of their existence in society.

I started conducting online sessions on soft skills, mental health and well-being, and spoken English for the community members along with my students. This provided them with productive engagement and gave them the confidence to apply for formal jobs. Apart from this, at school we conduct workshops for teachers from nursery till the 12th standard on how to avoid stereotyping and categorising students. These workshops are conducted by doctors. Sometimes, our students also try to join these workshops and create awareness around gender and sexuality along with basic human rights.

Personally, I make it a point to engage in conversations with friends and family around equal gender rights at social gatherings, and raising children to be respectful citizens. A lot of my friends are open to being allies now and respect people's sexuality. They even ask me questions to know more about the community and their rights. I engage my toddler in gender neutral story books and also sing rhymes where gender is not stereotyped. An example of one such rhyme is: 'A spoon runs away with another spoon instead of a dish'.

I also believe in having open dialogues with my child because it clears up a lot of doubts in her mind at an early age. I tell her that some children have two mothers or two fathers instead of always having a mother and a father like she has. In this way, she will grow up to respect everyone and not participate in bullying at any point in life. I have also introduced her to gender fluid colouring books in which girls are riding dinosaurs, running bike repair shops and boys are performing ballet, playing with doll houses, have long hair, and some kids on wheelchairs are dancing too! As parents and adults, it is our responsibility to choose what is best for our children while giving them the right upbringing. This lays a strong foundation rather than avoiding discussions on uncomfortable issues with them thinking they will learn on their own when they grow up. This will only confuse them.

I would urge you to put yourself in others' shoes (community members). Once you experience what it feels like to be called 'abnormal', 'not natural', or feel discarded from the rest of the society, only then you will understand the hardships. Fighting for the rights that one is already born with can be distressing and highly painful. It is important for each one of us to take up the responsibility to spread awareness about the history of the existence of the LGBT+ community because many of us feel this is a foreign/western culture import whereas, it is very much Indian.

Please make sex education and gender discussions normal at home and educational spaces. Many feel children's minds get polluted with these talks. While I do understand there is an apt age for everything, I also feel there is a right age to introduce these topics subtly to the children in different ways that will not harm, but help them. The more you talk about these, the less children will depend on the internet for answers.

We must adapt and change with the times. Let us raise empathetic human beings with open minds. Lastly, to all the young adults and kids—please believe in yourselves. There may be many who will pull you down, will hush you or even tell you that you are wrong, but you must believe in yourself. There is a lot of help you can take from counsellors and your loved ones. It is important to talk it out and have healthy conversations with people you trust. Believe in the power of conversations.

It is important for educational institutions and workplaces to introduce queer role models, to include personalities and fictional characters from the community and talk about them.

It is also important to create jobs and hire members from the community in every work space to create allies, as access to LGBT+ people will help de-stigmatise them, and increased engagement will lead to better understanding and allyship.

Acknowledgements

"Gratitude is when memory is stored in the heart and not in the mind." LIONEL HAMPTON

Equally, is a celebration of allyship & token of gratitude to all allies of the LGBT+ community.

To all 45 authors, who took the time out, to so eloquently share their deeply personal ally stories, with us. We thank you for your commitment to inclusion, we are truly honoured to be able to chronicle it.

Especially grateful to Rupa Publications, Dibakar Ghosh, and the team for making this dream a reality, for supporting us every step of the way, and enabling us to etch the journey of LGBT+ allyship through this wonderful piece of literature.

We would like to extend our gratitude to our industry partner, FICCI. Special thanks to Dilip and the team for the continued partnership and support.

Our gratitude to Sharif Rangnekar for being a pillar of strength, for his unwavering support and advice, for connecting the dots, for sharing a laugh, and for making this a memorable journey.

It has been a long winding road that got us here, Pride Circle's inclusivity mission has been made possible by the immense support of our well-wishers. We are thankful to you Keshav Suri, Parmesh Shahani, Zainab Patel for being such amazing allies to Pride Circle.

We wish there were more space for us to list all the names, of the people who have been there and made a difference in our lives and Pride Circle. To you we extend our deepest gratitude; without all your love and support, we would not have made it this far. All the partner organizations, companies, NGOs, Community Organizations, Embassies, Schools & Colleges, Social Media Groups, the many volunteers, every single one of you, we remain indebted to your kindness and generosity.

To the wonderful people at Pride Circle who have become family, for joining us and allowing us to live our true selves, every single day.

Our families have played a vital role in anything and everything, and remain our pillars of strength. A big thank you to all our family members for standing by us and steadfastly supporting our decision to move from the corporate world to embark on this beautiful journey, we call the Pride Circle.

Thank You, everyone!